MW01132221

God and the World's Arrangement

Readings from Vedānta and Nyāya Philosophy of Religion

God and the World's Arrangement

Readings from Vedānta and Nyāya Philosophy of Religion

Translated, with Introduction and Explanatory Notes, by

Nirmalya Guha

Matthew Dasti

Stephen Phillips

Hackett Publishing Company, Inc.
Indianapolis/Cambridge

Printed in the United States of America

24 23 22 21 1 2 3 4 5 6 7

For further information, please address
Hackett Publishing Company, Inc.
P.O. Box 44937
Indianapolis, Indiana 46244-0937

www.hackettpublishing.com

Cover design by Brian Rak
Composition by Aptara, Inc.

Library of Congress Control Number: 2020945950

ISBN-13: 978-1-62466-958-3 (cloth)
ISBN-13: 978-1-62466-957-6 (pbk.)

The paper used in this publication meets the minimum requirements of American National Standard for Information Sciences—Permanence of Paper for Printed Library Materials, ANSI Z39.48–1984.

∞

Contents

Acknowledgments

This book began with a guest lecture given by Nirmalya Guha in an upper-division philosophy course, Natural Theology East and West, at the University of Texas at Austin, when he was a Fulbright fellow there. Guha sketched out the argument of Śaṅkara that is presented here for a team-taught audience that included the professors of record for the course, Daniel Bonevac and Stephen Phillips. We two, Guha and Phillips, then began reading together the Sanskrit text that Guha used as the principal source for his presentation, along with the commentaries published in J. L. Shastri's edition of *Brahmasūtra-Śaṅkarabhāṣyam*. The two of us noticed how astute was the commentary of Vācaspati. Both of us already had great respect for Śaṅkara as a philosopher and reasoner of the very first order. We decided to translate their combined argument, which deserves wider readership. Soon after, we invited Matthew Dasti to join our project, and the three of us decided to include Vācaspati's theistic argument from his commentary on the *Nyāya-sūtra*.

All three of us are sanskritists as well as philosophy professionals. This volume has benefited by having three sets of eyes on the text, focused on the twin criteria of readability and accuracy. Guha and Phillips are the primary translators for Chapter 1. Dasti and Phillips are the primary translators for Chapter 2. The primary author of Appendix A is Phillips, while the primary translators for Appendix B are Dasti and Phillips. But all three of us are responsible for the text in full.

Nirmalya Guha wishes to thank his colleagues Stephen Phillips and Matthew Dasti as well as his friend Vinita Chandra.

Matthew Dasti wishes to thank his colleagues Nirmalya Guha and Stephen Phillips. He would also like to thank his family for their love and encouragement, as well as his colleagues in the philosophy department at Bridgewater State University for their unfailing support. He dedicates this work to his longtime friend and teacher, Edwin Bryant.

Stephen Phillips thanks his two colleagues along with his wife Hope for general support and encouragement. He also thanks the philosophy department of the University of Texas at Austin for permitting team teaching with Daniel Bonevac, and especially Professor Bonevac himself for his interests and insights into many areas of Indian philosophy and, in particular, the arguments presented here. Bonevac and Phillips have now taught Natural Theology East and West twice, and Phillips would like also to thank the two groups of students who have taken the course for their help in appreciating this and other arguments examined there.

Collectively, we are grateful to Tristan Johnson for reading portions of the manuscript and offering helpful feedback. Special thanks to Brian Rak and the team at Hackett for taking on the project and shepherding it to completion.

January 2020

Introduction

This book is motivated by an increased interest in non-Western topics and views within the contemporary philosophy of religion. No academic philosopher these days would deny that beyond the Western traditions, there is much that is worthy of study and investigation. However, this acknowledgment is not the same thing as a real engagement in informed, cosmopolitan inquiry. The remedy is not simply to urge that certain Eastern classics be read. Translations are sparse and often far from friendly to the uninitiated. People interested in the arguments are commonly stymied by contextual peculiarities and unfamiliar translation practices in indology, sinology, and so on. Furthermore, many classics, especially in the later Indian tradition, remain untranslated. Teachers looking for something accurate but also accessible to students in philosophy classes often have to rely on a summary presentation in some scholar's own voice, rather than the actual voice of any Eastern theorist.

Our goal here has been to provide materials from classical Indian philosophy that will help students and teachers move away from reliance on summaries alone, facilitating a direct engagement with primary texts. Our sense is that materials are needed through which non-Western voices can speak on issues that are meaningful now, materials that employ terminology familiar in contemporary thought. We have therefore aimed to provide useful translations of primary texts within the philosophy of religion. One challenge we faced is the enormity of the set of candidates. As runs an old saw, much Indian philosophy has some sort of connection to religion. And many religious texts, such as the *Bhagavad-gītā* and the sermons of the Buddha, have important philosophical themes. With the glut of possible source materials, any selection is somewhat arbitrary. But focusing on arguments about the existence of God narrows the field.[1] Our selections address whether or not

1 We use a range of theological terms to talk about an ultimate reality purported to be in some way the fundamental cause of the world. For the thinkers here, terms translated as "God" include *brahman*—Brahman according to Vedāntins being the ultimate material and agential cause of the universe—as well as *īśvara*, "the Lord,"

there exists a creator who stands as an agential cause of the world. Even on this theme, there are many texts fit to be translated and explored. Ours is but a representative portion of classical Indian contributions to a central question of natural theology: Are there successful arguments for the existence of such a creator God?

The readings translated here present arguments for an omniscient, creative being called *īśvara* ("the Lord"), but one is taken from Vedānta, which is primarily an exegetical school, and the other from Nyāya, which is primarily a school relying on reasoning. In Part 1, the text is from the *Brahma-sūtra* (also called the *Vedānta-sūtra*), 2.2.1–10, arguing that the fundamental cause of the world is sentient. The section comes from the treatise's "Chapter on Argument," which is devoted to conflicts with rival world views. The primary opponent is the Vedic ("Hindu")[2] school called Sāṃkhya, which holds that the world arises from insentient primordial matter, unfolding according to its own nature. The passage from the *Brahma-sūtra* is elucidated by the commentaries of Śaṅkara (fl. 710 CE) and Vācaspati (fl. 960 CE), two leading thinkers within Advaita or "Non-dual" Vedānta, whose impact was far-reaching not only with respect to other Vedāntic subschools but also in other traditions. The two argue that no primordial nature or matter could unfold into the marvelous diversity of the world without superintending agency.

Part 2 presents Vācaspati again, but wearing a different hat and arguing for *īśvara*'s existence in a distinct work and school, through his comments on the *Nyāya-sūtra*. The *Nyāya-sūtra* is the foundational text for the long-running tradition and school of Nyāya. Like other philosophers flying the Nyāya banner, Vācaspati presupposes that the material cause of the universe is not a unitive "stuff" like Sāṃkhya's primordial matter (*pradhāna*) or Vedānta's Brahman but rather atoms of distinct types. He argues that the macro structures we experience could come together only through the effort of conscious agency. This holds, he says, for all structured effects, whether

---

who is conceived by Nyāya philosophers similarly to the God of much Western natural theology. But see Nicholson, "Hindu Disproofs of God": 612–13 for the challenges associated with the term "God" when translating from Sanskritic sources.

2 The term "Hindu" is problematic for several reasons, yet it is often used to describe literary, cultural, and religious traditions that see themselves as inheritors of the Veda and of practices of Vedic culture, as distinguished from the Buddhists, Jainas, and others who reject the Veda and its allied culture.

artifacts like pots or naturally formed composites like human bodies, trees, and mountains. The latter require nonhuman agency, he argues, and the best candidate is *īśvara*, an omniscient and omnipresent Lord. The inference is opposed by a number of atheist voices, centrally Buddhist and Mīmāṃsaka (Hindu Ritualists), echoed in Vācaspati's responses to objections. Select passages from his argument, along with commentary by other Nyāya philosophers, may be found in Chapter 6 of Dasti and Phillips 2017. But here we include the entirety of Vācaspati's comprehensive argument for *īśvara*. By coupling Vācaspati's works on Vedānta and on Nyāya we hope to make it possible for a wide swath of his work to be pondered, little of which is currently accessible despite Vācaspati's importance for the whole of classical Indian philosophical thought.

By including a substantial discussion of Sāṃkhya in Part 1, and including translations of arguments against God in Appendix B, we also hope to help the reader become familiar with some of India's most prominent challenges to theism.

Part 1 of the volume is first largely because of historical ordering. Śaṅkara predates Vācaspati, who indeed comments upon him. As such, Part 2, which focuses on Vācaspati and Nyāya, naturally comes second. Part 1 does require a bit more conceptual scaffolding for the novice to make sense of Sāṃkhya and Advaita Vedānta, and we provide such scaffolding in the introduction to Part 1 and in Appendix A. Readers interested in jumping right into the theism/atheism debate in a streamlined way, however, may consider first reading Part 2 and Appendix B, and then moving on to Part 1 and Appendix A.

Inference and Technical Terms of Debate

The authors translated here presuppose a distinct vocabulary for philosophical debate, one that stands at the end of a millennium of philosophical disputes. Speculation about an ultimate reality can be found in the Veda, India's earliest text (some parts of it as old as 1500 BCE). But philosophy, even in the broad sense, is not pronounced in the Veda, which is comprised of poetry, hymns to various gods and goddesses, and liturgical material in appendices. In the Upaniṣads and the sermons of the Buddha (c. 500 BCE), in contrast, there is vigorous debate about various issues of metaphysics.

Thinkers in the later classical period (from about 100 BCE) take up a range of positions, usually inherited or adapted from the early speculations, and progressively apply logical tools to support those positions. This holds for theistic hypotheses as well as for many other controversial issues. Let us review a basic argument pattern repeatedly used in classical texts. Following this, we will consider some of the primary fallacies or ways that arguments were thought to fail by our thinkers.

For an individual, inference is the process whereby something not directly perceived becomes known on the basis of evidence. In a stock example, if a person S sees a distant hill with smoke, then S knows that there is fire there, given that S already knows that wherever there is smoke, there is fire. In this case, S neither sees the fire (that would be perception), nor learns about it from someone else (that would be testimony). But S knows it is there because smoke is an indicator of fire. In ordinary life, inferences occur constantly and automatically as a person navigates her environment. But should she need to prove what she's inferred to another person, she would have to verbalize the inferential process, mentioning both the indicator (smoke) and the target (fire), along with their invariable relationship (wherever there is smoke, there is fire). Her inference for herself thus becomes an argument for others, a series of steps from premises to conclusion, meant to show the truth to someone else.

The argument form is as follows.

> The hill (the *subject* of the inference) is fiery (fieriness is the *property to be proved*),
> because it is smoky (smokiness is the *prover* property).
> Whatever is smoky is fiery, like a fiery kitchen hearth (an *example* supporting the general rule).

In classical Indian philosophy, the same word, *anumāna*, is used both for inferences for oneself and for those expressed as an argument to show something to another. The standard logical form and methodology used to prove something to an audience is modeled on the natural process of inference, but is also self-consciously elaborated and nuanced, with sensitivity to possible counterarguments and challenges.

In the context of argument or debate, we translate the terms for indicators (*sādhana*, *hetu*, *liṅga*) as "prover." In the stock argument from smoke to fire, for any particular subject, smokiness is a prover of fieriness. Fieriness, then, is the "property to be proved." Thus the key terms of an argument are, first, what we are talking about, the *subject*, the bearer of the properties in question (here, the hill); second, the *prover* (here, smokiness); third, the *property to be proved* (here, fieriness); and fourth, a supporting *example* illustrating inductive support for the invariable tie between the prover and the property to be proved (here a fiery kitchen hearth).

It is worth dwelling on the importance of the example. The most general purpose of an example is to provide a noncontroversial instance of the relation between the *prover* and the *property to be proved*. In the argument above, by experience a person knows that smoke indicates fire, and the example of a fiery kitchen hearth provides an illustration of an inductive generalization from smoke to fire, an example that both parties can accept. A well-formed argument must therefore have an illustration—acceptable to both sides—of the general rule. A good argument must also be free from counterexamples, which would be cases of the prover without the property to be proved, and which undermine the general inductive rule that is being relied upon.

In classical Indian logic, the general tie between a prover and the property to be proved, which is known by inductive generalization, is called *vyāpti*. This is literally translated as "pervasion," and this is the standard translation of scholars working on classical Indian systems. A "pervasion" is a natural law or any other kind of invariable connection between anything F and any other thing G such that wherever there is an F there is also a G. Being F is *pervaded* by being G, just as something smoky must also be fiery. But however accurate it might be as a rendering of the Sanskrit word, we feel that the English term "pervasion" is too unfamiliar in logical usages to be of much use to philosophers who are not also sanskritists. This translation practice seems to us to substitute one unfamiliar technical term with another. So we tend to favor the well-known word "entailment" when the relation under consideration is that when something is F that proves that it is also G.

Given this schema, there are various recognizable ways that arguments can fail. It is possible that a prover is fallacious because there is no entailment relation between being F and being G. This is shown when there are counterexamples that illustrate the presence of the prover along with an absence of the property to be proved. For example, if one should claim that every politician is a crook, recognition of an honest politician would show that being a politician is not sufficient to prove the property at issue, being a crook, alleged for some candidate running for election. True entailment admits no counterexample. If a prover sometimes admits of counterexamples, it is called *deviant* (*anaikāntika*), and is fallacious, not a true prover. An even more significant failure occurs when a prover not only deviates but establishes the contradictory of the property to be proved. This sort of prover is called *contradictory* (*virodha*).

Another type of inference failure involves a prover not actually being present in the subject of the inference. What if one thinks she sees smoke over a distant hill, but the object she sees is actually dust thrown up by the wind? This would mean that there could be no genuine inference to fire, since the prover cited is not actually a feature of the hill she is talking about. Such a prover would be *unestablished* (*asiddha*), and the argument would fail.

Yet another type of failure occurs when the property to be proved is not actually present in the example. Should one argue that "People who purchase Japanese vehicles, like this Honda Accord, do not support business in the USA," the error would be committed, since most Hondas purchased in the United States are in fact assembled there. As such, this example is *lacking the property to be proved* (*sādhya-hīna*).

Summarizing the above, the innovative Buddhist logician Dignāga (480–540 CE) identified three features of a good prover: (i) being present in the subject, (ii) being present in the example, and (iii) not being present in any counterexample.

A distinct type of misfire occurs when an inference is beset by an *undercutting defeater* (*upādhi*). This happens when something that seems to be a good prover holds true only when an additional property is present, a property unrecognized by the reasoner, not noticed until a critic of the inference points it out. Such an extra property, the *upādhi*, undermines the status of the prover on its own. In a contemporary medical example, one who experiences a certain pain or discomfort every time she eats bread may surmise that gluten is bad for people to eat. But her friend in medical school could respond that there is an *inferential undercutting defeater*, which undermines her presumption of an entailment from gluten to discomfort like hers. The entailment holds only when the individual also has celiac disease. Gluten by itself does not entail the discomfort.

Reasoning about God in Nyāya and Vedānta

Natural theology in India is usually associated with the Nyāya school. Thinkers from at least the time of the Nyāya philosopher Uddyotakara (c. 540–600 CE) championed a number of arguments meant to prove the existence of a creator, *īśvara*. For example:

> Primordial matter, atoms, and karma have to be directed by a conscious agent before they can function, since they are insentient, like an axe. As axes, due to insentience, cut only when directed by an axeman, so too do insentient things, such as primordial nature, atoms, and karma, come to function. Therefore, they too are directed by a conscious agent as a cause. (Uddyotakara, *Nyāya-vārttika* 4.1.21; trans. Dasti and Phillips, *The Nyāya-sūtra*, 120–21)

An inference like this is usually the first word, not the last, in discussions of controversial issues in philosophical treatises, presented with an eye to provoking criticisms and replies. Typically, an author advances an argument to frame an issue and then goes on to identify points of contention. Elaborating and defending the argument from objections, historical and imagined, fills out the text. For generations after Uddyotakara, sophisticated critiques were put forth by rival thinkers (see Appendix B), who framed criticisms according to the inferential lexicon outlined above. Vācaspati's argument in Part 2 responds to the criticisms in the course of his comprehensive argument for God.

Knowing that Nyāya is famous for logic and epistemology, one might expect that in embracing theism the school would pioneer a natural, rational theology. But what about Vedānta, a school that is also theistic but that reveres sacred testimony in the form of the Upaniṣads? Here the question of rational theology is complex. Surprisingly, non-Advaita, realist schools of Vedānta, which are invariably theistic, often try to problematize Nyāya's natural theology. Some proffer sustained refutations of its arguments (for example, Rāmānuja, *Śrī-Bhāṣya* 1.1.3). This is not because they oppose a theistic version of the world's creation, but rather because of their contention that inference alone, without revelation, is capable of generating knowledge of Brahman. Not unlike theistic criticisms of the arguments for

God proffered in early modern Europe,[3] these Vedāntins do not wish to undermine theistic belief but rather to stress the primacy of sacred tradition as fundamental.

Within the broad context of all the Vedāntic subschools, the passage we translate in Part 1 (*Brahma-sūtra* 2.2.1–10) is perhaps exceptional in its championing of unaided reasoning to defend the existence of God. It constitutes the fourth of four separate refutations of Sāṃkhya in Śaṅkara's *Brahma-sūtra* commentary. The first three (found in his commentaries on 1.1.5–11, 18; 1.4.1–28; and 2.1.1–11) are concerned with the proper interpretation of Upaniṣadic texts and the proper weighing of that testimony along with other sources of knowledge. In the selection translated here, Śaṅkara and, following him, Vācaspati, insist that a refutation of Sāṃkhya atheism be shown by reasoning alone, independent of Upaniṣadic revelation. Advocates of Sāṃkhya have their own proof texts. Hence there is call for rational argumentation to prove a conscious, efficient cause of the universe, against a theory of an insentient origin. In other words, our two authors allege that a true Vedāntin philosopher should criticize the atheistic idea by reason alone, without appeal to scripture, and may well need to do so in order to show certain opponents the truth. Thus, Vācaspati writes:

> It's wrong to hold that the Sāṃkhya inference could simply be dismissed because it is opposed by the statements of traditional scripture. For Sāṃkhya and similar schools are pioneered by "all-knowing" sages, and as such, have sacred traditions comparable to the Vedic traditions. Their arguments cannot be dismissed out of hand as if they were lion replicas.

A lion replica is not frightening when one realizes that it's a dupe. Some Vedāntins may argue that similarly, a Sāṃkhya argument may be dismissed out of hand when one realizes that it is not authentically Vedāntic. But Vācaspati says that move is not permissible, since Sāṃkhya was pioneered by sages conventionally held to be all-knowing. Relying on testimony exclusively,

3 See, e.g., Newman, *Fifteen Sermons*.

whether Upaniṣadic or not, would lead to a stalemate of competing authorities. The only way out is rational argument. Thus, Śaṅkara writes:

> Seeing that esteemed systems like Sāṃkhya have been accepted by great people who have set out to articulate the right view, some gullible folks may be led to think that those systems should be adopted in order to have the right view. Similarly, some folk may have faith in those wrong philosophies because of the profundity of the arguments that they think have been put forth by all-knowing sages. Therefore, in this section we proceed to show that these views fail to deliver the essential truth.

Śaṅkara is less charitable in tone, but the main point remains that for Vedāntins there is a place for rational theology if the hope is to convince those who do not share their presuppositions and commitments. For them, the best source of knowledge of ultimate reality and the cause of the universe may be Upaniṣadic revelation, but reason can play an important role in adjudicating disputes. The tendency among some scholars to refuse Śaṅkara the full status of "philosopher" often seems motivated by the way his commitments apparently rank inference below sacred testimony. Our view is different: reasoning can shine gloriously, whatever the reasoner's views on the precise status of revelation.

Note on the Translations

In this book, we have tried to adhere to the translator's ethics outlined in the Introduction to Dasti and Phillips, *The Nyāya-sūtra*, which recognizes the pedagogical duty to provide clarity as well as the philological to be accurate and the philosophical to be critically minded. Most of all, we have tried to make the texts as accessible as possible to undergraduates without sacrificing fidelity. Use of parentheses and brackets to restore material dropped in Sanskrit by ellipsis is minimal. Implied ideas that would have been obvious to a classical reader as part of what's being asserted are made explicit in English. Our renderings are thus aimed at the sense of the texts and sometimes disregard surface grammar.

A feature of Indian scholastic philosophy that stands out to new readers is its distinctive style of dialectical exchange. Authors commonly signal transitions from opponent to proponent and vice versa by certain "discourse markers" that do no more than show a shift of voice. Rarely are the objectors identified by name or creed. Furthermore, objectors are not always invented to express the views of a particular school or camp. Sometimes, an objector poses a rhetorical question that sets up a qualification to a thesis. In other instances, objectors are used to paraphrase or quote arguments given by actual historical individuals. As a rule, we use the heading "Objection" simply to flag a discourse shift, and further detail is provided according to context as necessary. In other words, objections as a group should not be thought of as representing monolithic opposition throughout a passage, but rather rival views coming from many corners and camps.

In order to maintain our own focus on the claims that ground the commentaries, sūtras are rendered in **boldface**, including quotations of sūtras, whether partial or complete, by the commentators. Our own translators' comments will be interspersed throughout the text and distinguished by *italicized* font.

Part 1 and Appendix A follow the Sanskrit edition of Śaṅkara, *Brahma-sūtra-bhāṣya* (edited by J. L. Shastri, 1980). Part 2 follows Vācaspati Miśra, *Nyāya-vārttika-tātparya-ṭīkā* (edited by Anantalal Thakur, 1996). Appendix B follows Kumārila Bhaṭṭa, *Ślokavārttika of Śrī Kumārila Bhaṭṭa* (edited by Swami Dwarikadas Shastri, 1978) and Dharmakīrti, *Pramāṇavārttika* (edited by Swami Dwarikadas Shastri, 1968). Other editions that have been consulted are listed in the Bibliography.

Part One

Śaṅkara's Theistic Argument in His *Brahma-sūtra* Commentary, with Subcommentary by Vācaspati Miśra

Vedānta and the *Brahma-sūtra*

The translation below is a selection from the school of Vedānta, which takes its name from the combination of the terms *veda* and *anta*. Four ancient compositions, known collectively as "Veda" or the "Vedas," are counted as revelation according to a variety of Hindu traditions. These traditions see the ancient Vedic culture as their great religious and intellectual ancestor. What counts as Vedic is complicated, however, when we take a close look at ancient Indian literature. The Upaniṣads are appendices to the Veda (some as old as 800 BCE), and there we find the first real blossoming of sustained Indian philosophical speculation. The Sanskrit word *anta* means *end*. The Upaniṣads are called "Vedānta" because they are added to the end of each of the four Vedas and thus comprise the final parts of each text. Like its English counterpart, *anta* may also mean *goal* or *fulfillment*, and this meaning is also present when the Upaniṣads are spoken of as "Vedānta." Vedāntins, those philosophers devoted to understanding the Upaniṣads, insist that they are the fulfillment and culmination of Vedic teachings in that they go beyond ritual practice and ordinary morality to inform us about a true self (*ātman*), a deepest essence, which is linked to the Ultimate Reality, Brahman.

As a mature school in the middle and later classical periods, Vedānta is comprised of a family of traditions and subschools devoted to a systematic understanding of Brahman as taught in the Upaniṣads and some other texts, most importantly, the *Bhagavad-gītā*. As a systematic worldview, Vedānta may be said to be inaugurated in the *Brahma-sūtra* (c. 400 CE in its final redaction) attributed to the legendary figure Bādarāyaṇa. Sūtra literature is in general made up of pithy statements, usually single sentences, that collectively provide a comprehensive understanding of a topic. The sūtra genre ranges widely, from philosophy (the *Brahma-sūtra*, *Nyāya-sūtra*, *Vaiśeṣika-sūtra*, etc.) and hermeneutics (the *Mīmāṃsā-sūtra*) to yoga practice (the *Yoga-sūtra*) and crafts (*Śilpa-śāstra*) and even the art of romance (the *Kāma-sūtra*). Sūtra texts commonly serve as root texts for the several philosophical schools, with each new generation of thinkers providing their own explications while also expanding the work of previous commentator-philosophers. Commentaries are a primary way that classical thinkers develop their views, especially in the formative period of a school. Commentators in all areas typically look back to a root text and earlier commentators for direction while responding to controversies of their own times.

The *Brahma-sūtra* differentiates Vedānta from Mīmāṃsā, the main school of Vedic exegesis. The two schools are akin in that they both recognize the Veda as sacred revelation, but Vedānta focuses on the Upaniṣads, while Mīmāṃsā is concerned with the proper conduct of Vedic rituals. The *Brahma-sūtra* distinguishes itself by declaring Brahman to be its primary topic of inquiry. This is opposed to the Mīmāṃsā focus on the ritual portion of the Veda, with its injunctions about right ritual performance and, in general, the right ways to live. The *Brahma-sūtra* adopts Mīmāṃsā's epistemology of scripture as self-certifying and authoritative within its own sphere. But it contends that that sphere is distinct in the case of the Upaniṣads: the province of Upaniṣadic texts is Brahman, along with how we may become aware of Brahman. The rites and actions prescribed by the ritual portion of the Veda are, according to Vedāntins, overridden by a superior path of knowledge, whereby the embodied can come to know Brahman, intellectually and in direct experience. The direct experience is sometimes said to be *mukti*, "liberation," the knower being liberated from rebirth.

The *Brahma-sūtra* has less subtle quarrels with other classical schools, although regarding Sāṃkhya (the school of "Enumeration"), scriptural interpretation remains an issue. Important portions of the early Upaniṣads do, in fact, resonate with a Sāṃkhya understanding of nature. Sāṃkhya proposes that there is a primordial nature which contains in unmanifest form all worldly manifestations. Moreover, Sāṃkhya has a hierarchical psychology of an embodied self and its faculties, ranging from reason to sense organs and organs of action, that coheres with many Upaniṣadic teachings. Despite these resonances, the *Brahma-sūtra* is intent on integrating its psychology and the metaphysics with a fundamentally Brahman-centered worldview, and disputes the contention that Sāṃkhya philosophy is taught in the Upaniṣads. The *Brahma-sūtra* further disputes Sāṃkhya on non-scriptural grounds, especially over metaphysics, as is evident in the selection here, a theistic argument directed against atheistic Sāṃkhya in the second book of the *Brahma-sūtra*. The selection is but one small sample of Vedāntic philosophic literature, which engages in disputes with several schools including Nyāya and Vaiśeṣika and subschools of Jainism and Buddhism.

Our passage targets the Sāṃkhya notion of primordial matter as the ultimate cause of the world, as an insentient primordial stuff. Vedānta contends, in contrast, that Brahman, the material cause of everything, is not only sentient but an original agential cause bringing about our world of finite diversities. Here, first, sans commentary, are the sūtras that we examine below.

2.2.1 And because the world's arrangement would be impossible, the argument that would establish an insentient cause of the universe is not legitimate.

2.2.2 And because of action, the Sāṃkhya primordial matter cannot be proved.

2.2.3 If it is argued that primordial matter can act, just like milk or water, the reply is that in those cases too there is guidance by a conscious being.

2.2.4 Primordial matter could not unfold on its own, since (i) there would be nothing in that state which is different from it and (ii) it does not depend upon anything else.

2.2.5 And primordial matter is not spontaneously active in the manner of grass and the like because grass does not change into milk anywhere else than in a cow's stomach.

2.2.6 Even if it were conceded (that it could move spontaneously), primordial matter still would not act on its own because it has no purpose.

2.2.7 If your contention is that a *puruṣa* (pure self) moves primordial matter like a magnet, similar problems remain.

2.2.8 Furthermore, subordination (of one mode to another) is impossible.

2.2.9 Moreover, (the defects remain) if you make a different inference, since primordial matter is divorced from the power of consciousness.

2.2.10 Furthermore, because of inconsistencies, the view is contradictory.

Śaṅkara and Vācaspati Miśra

While the gist of the ideas in the sūtras above may be evident, fine-grained understanding is sometimes difficult, or even impossible, without commentary. Doubtless the earliest commentaries on the *Brahma-sūtra* were oral. Śaṅkara (fl. 710 CE) is the author of the oldest written commentary that has come down to us (palm-leaf manuscripts had to be recopied every century or be lost), but he mentions predecessors whose texts, if any, are not extant. The historical importance of Śaṅkara is difficult to overstate. In general, he stands as the major figure in the Vedānta school, whose work is either the starting point for future reflection, according to Advaita ("Non-dual") subschools, or, for opposed subschools, the mistaken opponent whom one must correct.

Many legends have grown up around Śaṅkara, the premier Advaita Vedāntin. He probably was born in Kerala, though some say Tamil Nadu. He is purported to have become a renouncer, *sannyāsin*, at an early age, and also to have become quite learned while very young, writing voluminously and lecturing all over India. Śaṅkara is said to have founded a famous order of renunciants as well as temple traditions at the four corners of the subcontinent, defeating Buddhists and other rivals in open debate. Tradition has it that he died at the age of thirty-two, having composed not only his voluminous *Brahma-sūtra-bhāṣya* (*Commentary on the Brahma-sūtra*) but also commentaries on several Upaniṣads and the *Bhagavad-gītā*. Non-commentarial works attributed to Śaṅkara—including *A Thousand Teachings* (*Upadeśa-sahasrī*) as well as some that are actually by followers—make him out as principally a spiritual preceptor, a guru. That may well be the best general characterization, but it does not preclude counting him as a philosopher too. Śaṅkara is traditionally known as a living saint but also as an astute reasoner. In our selection, we find him refuting the Sāṃkhya view of the origin of the universe as he advances an argument for Brahman, who is conceived as a conscious agent.

Śaṅkara's status as a philosopher proper is sometimes controversial among scholars and modern champions of classical Indian philosophy, some viewing him as a philosopher par excellence, others as more of an exegete. His commentary presented here, where the existence of Brahman is purportedly proved, shows him as a philosopher rather than an exegete. We admit that for the larger debate the selection of the passage is skewed in favor of philosophy. Be that as it may, we expect readers to come away with respect for Śaṅkara as a reasoner, whatever the best label for his corpus as a whole might be.

Vācaspati Miśra (fl. 960 CE) is said to have lived in Mithilā, in what is now Bihar. He is also special historically but for a different reason: Vācaspati is one of a very few classical authors to write under different scholastic banners. Indeed, his texts fly not two but five flags: Mīmāmsā, Sāṃkhya, Yoga, and Nyāya, in addition to Vedānta.[1] A challenge in understanding Vācaspati's own voice as a philosopher is determining which of the views and traditions he personally endorses. Scholars argue that his commentary on Śaṅkara's *Brahma-sūtra-bhāṣya* was his last and most heartfelt work. It is called the *Bhāmatī*, and is said to be named for his wife, who, instead of a line of children, received a different kind of immortality: fame. Vācaspati also wrote a commentary on the *Yoga-sūtra*, where his persona seems less that of a yogin speaking from personal experience than that of a scholar explaining the philosophical system and psychology taken to underlie yoga practices. In our selections both here and in Part 2, he is clearly a philosophical theist, elaborating Śaṅkara's argument for the existence of Brahman and later, the Nyāya proof of *īśvara*, "the Lord." It is our opinion that Vācaspati is underappreciated as a creative thinker, but that is not something to argue here.[2] Vācaspati is responsible for pioneering advances in Nyāya theory in particular, including its rational theology, as well as for founding a distinct

1 For translations of some of Vācaspati's works apart from Vedānta and Nyāya, see Woods, *The Yoga Sūtras*; Vācaspati, *Tattva-kaumudi* (ed. and tr. Jha); and Vācaspati, *Tattva-bindu* (ed. and tr. Biardeau).

2 See Phillips, "Seeing from the Other's Point of View," for an argument for Vācaspati's originality as a creative philosopher, not merely a school-bound expositor of various texts.

subschool of Advaita Vedānta. In our selections, he shows a comprehensive, clear grasp of the philosophies of his times.

Advaita Vedānta

Advaita ("Non-dual") Vedānta, the school of Śaṅkara and Vācaspati, advocates a monism of non-dual consciousness, which it grounds in a specific reading of the Upaniṣads. A central teaching of the Upaniṣads is that the Brahman is "one without a second" and that it has "non-dual" awareness of itself.[3] The Vedāntic tradition has more than a dozen competing subschools who share an allegiance to the teaching of the Upaniṣads and the *Brahma-sūtra*. The subschools tend to be divided mainly according to their metaphysics of how the world (including individual persons) relates to Brahman. There is much variety in positions on the issue. Contemporary scholars make a broad, simple distinction between two major strands: Advaita, "Non-dual" Vedānta and "Theistic" Vedānta. The latter group is usually called "Theistic Vedānta" because it understands Brahman primarily as world creator, with the universe emanating under the Lord's direction. The emphasis with the Advaita subschool is on Brahman as a unifying ground of being and awareness. The world of multiplicity—including multiple individual selves—is held to be inexplicable to our minds if we try to figure out conceptually how our world of distinct individuals looks from the perspective of Brahman itself. This emphasis may be said to overshadow or diminish the theistic elements within Advaita, at least according to some readings. In any case, the term *anirvacanīya*, "inexplicability," is central, not so much as a word with Śaṅkara himself as with his immediate followers, who use it to capture one central thesis.[4] But Śaṅkara himself says explicitly in *A Thousand Teachings* (*Upadeśa-sahasrī* 1.1.18) that the world of "name and form" (*nāma-rūpa*) cannot be explained (*anirvacanīya*) in relation to the supreme self. We cannot understand from Brahman's perspective why our world appears.

3 *Bṛhadāraṇyaka Upaniṣad* 4.3.9 says that in sleep a person dreams by her "own light" and then becomes "self-illumined." Light is apparently picked as an analogy because light requires no source of illumination outside itself. A central Advaita claim is that pure consciousness is "non-dual," *a-dvaita*, that it knows itself by being itself.

4 Potter, *Encyclopedia of Indian Philosophies, vol. 3*, 80.

This inexplicability is in our (the translators') opinion the crucial Advaita tenet for understanding two commonly misunderstood notions in the system, *māyā* ("illusion") and *avidyā* ("spiritual ignorance"). Let us elaborate.

The way the world looks from Brahman's perspective cannot be known by us intellectually, according to Non-dualists. The difference between our perspective and the Absolute's is so radical that we may be said to live in "spiritual ignorance," *avidyā*, which is an ignorance so severe that it may be compared to an illusion. Advaita's rivals do not draw such a sharp line between the Absolute and us, finding features of our world to be derivative from the nature of Brahman. For example, matter is said to be the body of God, insofar as the Lord is the world-self and our minds are also broadly analogous to the mind of God. There is more continuity between the orders of reality for the "Theistic Vedāntins" than for the Non-dualists who find the central continuity to lie in our self-awareness of our own existence as conscious beings.

The divisions among the subschools should not be framed, however, as theism versus atheism, as our translation makes dramatically clear. Advaitins do accept a creator, an emanationist and agential primary cause. But they hold that viewing Brahman as a personal creator God requires a theoretic perspective that is influenced by the nature of all mentality as "spiritual ignorance," *avidyā*. Spiritual ignorance is a precondition of anything that presupposes multiplicity, including every instance of reasoning as well as scripture itself! Nevertheless, given our intellectual perspectives as human individuals informed by reason and revelation, Vedānta holds that when we try to make sense of this world of multiplicity, it is best thought of as having Brahman as both its material and its agential first cause.

How exactly Brahman relates to the world other than as the underpinning of the individual self is intellectually mysterious, according to Advaita. Śaṅkara maintains that the best view is, as the Upaniṣads teach, that Brahman is a conscious agent "loosing forth" the world out of itself (and this is clearly stated in the very second sūtra of the *Brahma-sūtra*). In the Introduction to his *Brahma-sūtra-bhāṣya* and at sūtra 1.4.14, he says that the differences within various accounts of the creation found in the Upaniṣads do not much matter, since the details are not important. What is important is that they agree that the cause of the world is the "omniscient Lord, the Self of all." We need a worldview to guide our actions and aspirations, and according to Śaṅkara the worldview to be adopted is the emanationist theism of the Upaniṣads. In our reading, all Vedānta philosophy is theist, although there is great divergence among subschools in emphasizing the role of *īśvara*, "the Lord," in metaphysics and praxis. The scholarly habit of distinguishing sharply between Non-dual Vedānta and Theistic Vedānta is thus misleading (see Appendix A for further discussion).

Vedānta versus Sāṃkhya

The main opponent to Vedānta in the section we translate below is Sāṃkhya, the school of "Enumeration." As a general approach to metaphysics, Sāṃkhya is ancient and enigmatic, less a discrete school of thought than a primordial Indian practice of categorizing various features of reality into a distinct number of fundamental principles. Far from there being a single school in ancient India, there were various Sāṃkhya traditions, and more fundamentally a plethora of ways that Sāṃkhya methodologies influenced Indian thinkers of every stripe, in disciplines like metaphysics and theology, but also psychology and medicine. Beyond this, Sāṃkhya was associated with meditational practices of disidentification, where an individual articulates these fundamental principles in order to disidentify with them, leaving the pure conscious self as the remainder.

By Śaṅkara's time, there had emerged a distinct school of Sāṃkhya thought, with specific positions on most of the major philosophical issues. This version of Sāṃkhya is called "classical Sāṃkhya" and finds expression in the *Sāṃkhya-kārikā* (c. 350–450 CE). In this text, arguments are put forth to prove the existence of primordial matter as the source of the world. These are like theistic cosmological arguments, but instead of God they aim to establish an insentient prime matter out of which everything evolves. Śaṅkara cites these arguments in his commentary, and we reconstruct one of them below. Sāṃkhya challenges Vedānta principally because the school denies conscious agency as a fundamental feature of reality. Strictly speaking, all change takes place not only within but also exclusively through instigations of matter, which is viewed as having an innate tendency to unfold in certain ways. Consciousness, too, is real, but it is fundamentally inactive; each of us is merely a witness to material fluctuations and otherwise disconnected from them. The original creative force is thus neither God nor a God-like being, but rather primordial matter, unfolding on its own. The prime matter is called *pradhāna*, "the primary," or sometimes *avyakta*, "the unmanifest" (compared to the manifest world of finite things). Against this idea, Vedāntins contend that creation requires an agent.

To understand Sāṃkhya reasoning, let us consider one argument for primordial matter, the argument *from delimited measurement*[5]: effects in general are delimited by measurements, emerging from a cause that is less limited. For example, a clay pot is much more precisely defined than the clay out of which it is made. It is more measured and specified. A lump of clay is less defined than a pot, less individualized. Of course, a lump of clay is also a product. So it must have come from something else, something less limited and less defined, which would itself come from something still less limited and less defined. The sequence must have a terminus, a beginning point. For Sāṃkhya philosophers, it is prime matter, a primordial stuff of the universe, infinite materiality in its purest and grandest potentiality. Specifically, the *Sāṃkhya-kārikā* says (verses 14 and 15):

> It is inferred that the cause (*kāraṇa*) of diverse objects is the unmanifest. The reasons for this are: (i) the delimited nature of effects, (ii) the continuity between cause and effects, (iii) the emergence of effects depending on the potency of the cause.

Some of the further reasons will be explored in the translation and in comments on specific passages.

Classical Sāṃkhya philosophy is, in sum, atheistic, like modern materialism. The *pradhāna* evolves naturally. It does not need the guidance of a sentient being. Here are teachings from two more verses from the *Sāṃkhya-kārikā* (21, 57) to fill out the worldview:

> The union of the self and the *pradhāna* is meant for the liberation of the self and the objectification of the *pradhāna*. Their union is like the union of a blind person and a lame person. Creation emerges from their union. . . . Although cow milk is insentient, it flows for the sake of

---

5 See p. 16 of this volume.

> the calf's growth. Similarly, *pradhāna*, which is insentient, functions for the sake of the self's liberation.

The insentient *pradhāna* by nature has the ability to be experienced, that is, it has a kind of self-objectification. Matter is by nature active but insentient while the self is by nature inactive but sentient.

At some point during its sojourn though repeated birth and death, an individual looks for an exit. Sāṃkhya holds that one realizes that pain is experienced by the mind, which is ultimately a product of the prime matter. The self feels pain since it falsely identifies with the mind and body. No pain or pleasure belongs to the self as it is in itself. This realization brings about disconnection between the individual consciousness and matter. This is liberation. When a specific self gets liberated, the *pradhāna* stops functioning in relation to that person.

For our concerns, the main point is that since all these things happen naturally, no God is required in the system. Nobody needs to supervise the evolution of the *pradhāna*. Nobody has to trigger or stop it. Such is the Sāṃkhya atheism combated by our Vedāntins. To oppose the line of thinking, Śaṅkara and Vācaspati argue that various features of creation indicate conscious, intentional agency. Centrally, these are structured effects and initial activity. In both cases, they argue, conscious agency is required. They also respond to alleged counterexamples and give reasons why the Sāṃkhya view of undirected creation, driven by a primordial matter's inner telos, is incoherent.

Translation

Brahma-sūtra 2.2.1–10 with the complete commentary of Śaṅkara and select sub-commentary of Vācaspati Miśra.

§ § §

Sūtra 2.2.1. _racanā anupapatteś ca na anumānam_ |

And because the world's arrangement would be impossible, the argument that would establish an insentient cause of the universe is not legitimate.

Śaṅkara: This systematic study is commenced in order to determine the meaning of Vedāntic statements. It is not to establish or refute some thesis by argument alone, like the study of reasoning (*tarka-śāstra*). Nevertheless, those who would explain Vedāntic statements should disprove Sāṃkhya and similar views which stand opposed to the right view. It is for this purpose that a new section is commenced. Achieving certainty about the content of Vedānta is for the sake of having the right view. One's own position becomes firm through that certainty. Indeed, this is to be accomplished first, as it is more important than confuting another's position.

Vācaspati Miśra: It's wrong to hold that the Sāṃkhya inference could simply be dismissed because it is opposed by the statements of traditional scripture. For Sāṃkhya and similar schools are pioneered by "all-knowing" sages, and as such, have sacred traditions comparable to the Vedic traditions. Their arguments cannot be dismissed out of hand as if they were lion replicas. Since a contradiction between Sāṃkhya's view and Vedānta remains, a comprehensive account of Vedāntic statements about Brahman is not settled, which further entails that it is not possible to establish knowledge of what is ultimately true. In the absence of knowledge of what is ultimately true, there is no liberation. Therefore, it is entirely consistent with Vedāntic scholarship to illustrate the fallaciousness of opposed inferences on their own merit.

Objection: For those seeking liberation, determination of the right system is part of the path. Simply firming up one's own position is then all that one needs to do. What's the point of refuting others' positions, which may engender the adverse emotion of hatred on their part?

Śaṅkara: That's true as far as it goes. Nevertheless, there is such a need. Seeing that esteemed systems like Sāṃkhya have been accepted by great people who have set out to articulate the right view, some gullible folks may be led to think that those systems should be adopted in order to have the right view. Similarly, some folk may have faith in those wrong philosophies because of the profundity of the arguments that they think have been put forth by all-knowing sages. Therefore, in this section we proceed to show that these views fail to deliver the essential truth.

Vācaspati Miśra: Śaṅkara's point is that nonpartisan debate is directed toward discovery of truth. Yet without refutation of opponents' positions, certainty about truth would not be possible. Therefore, even someone who is unattached will refute opponents' positions, but not *because* the positions belong to someone else. It is thus not opposed to the spirit of debate that is free of personal attachment.

Vedānta is typically understood to be a school devoted to systematic exegesis of sacred texts like the Upaniṣads. As a rule, the right order in Vedāntic methodology is first to settle the correct views about Brahman as expressed in Upaniṣadic texts and then to go on to refute opposed positions. Otherwise, we would have no reference point whereby to see just what positions are opposed to Vedāntic teaching. But here our commentators are taking pains to argue that the independent refutation of other schools like Sāṃkhya is within the scope of legitimate Vedāntic practice. For Śaṅkara and Vācaspati, refutation of Sāṃkhya and other views is of paramount importance because unresolved contradiction between two views leaves us unsure of what to believe. Each view would have an at least prima facie origin in a knowledge source (here Vedāntic testimony for Vedānta and inference for Sāṃkhya). It is not obvious why the former should trump the latter even if it does. Worse than this, people may be led astray by attractive but false views.

Vācaspati's example of lion replicas is important: While one may be startled upon seeing a lion statue, upon realizing that it is a statue, one immediately dismisses it as being something unworthy of fear. A proponent of Vedānta may think that in the same way, as soon as one recognizes that views like Sāṃkhya are not consistent with Upaniṣadic texts, they may be rejected as false. But Vācaspati refuses to do this. The adherents of schools like Sāṃkhya often hold that their founders were sages with unique insights, and give them the epithet "all-knowing." Whether or not Vācaspati accepts such a status for these persons, he underscores that the matter cannot simply be settled by claiming that one side has spiritual authority and the other doesn't. Such would result in an impasse of conflicting authorities.

Vedānta may be a scriptural tradition, but there is a distinct role for philosophical argumentation in settling disputes.

Objection: In the sūtras, **Because seeing (i.e., consciousness) is attributed to the world's cause, the existence of *pradhāna* is not supported by the Upaniṣads** (*Brahma-sūtra* 1.1.5), as well as **And because of desire being attributed to the world's cause, the (Sāṃkhya) resort to inference is wrong** (*Brahma-sūtra* 1.1.18), and **By this reasoning, all systems explained as opposed to the Vedānta are explained (to be wrong)** (*Brahma-sūtra* 1.4.28), Sāṃkhya and other positions opposed to the Vedāntic teaching about the world's origin have already been rejected. What's the point of doing it again?

Śaṅkara: What has been done earlier, in the first chapter of the *Brahma-sūtra*, is limited to showing that the explanation of Upaniṣadic statements that is propounded by systems like Sāṃkhya is not correct. They put forth a false explanation in the course of making their arguments, suggesting that the Upaniṣads are consistent with their own view, and they use Vedāntic statements in order to establish their own positions. Here, in contrast, their arguments will be rejected on independent grounds, without reference to Upaniṣadic assertions. This is the difference.

Among these systems, the Sāṃkhya understanding is as follows: We find that in general, individual pots and other clay vessels have in common being made out of clay. Analogously, everything, every individual, whether inanimate or animate, has in common being made out of pleasure, pain, and delusion. That which is common everywhere is primordial matter (*pradhāna*), which is comprised of the three "modes" (*guṇas*), which have the character of pleasure, pain, and dullness respectively. Like clay, primordial matter is insentient. Just by its diverse intrinsic nature, it transforms, unfolding spontaneously to satisfy the purposes of the individual conscious being (*puruṣa*).

Similarly to the case of clay, an insentient primordial matter is also inferred for reasons that include the delimited nature of effects.[6]

6 See *Sāṃkhya-kārikā* 14–16 for a list of the provers given by Sāṃkhya to establish the existence of primordial matter. This specific argument is discussed in the introduction to Part 1, above.

Vācaspati Miśra: Sāṃkhya philosophers hold that whatever emerges in whatever form, from the macro to the micro, is found to have something as its material cause. For example, at all levels of their composition, things like pots and gold necklaces are made of clay and gold respectively, which serve as their material causes. Sāṃkhya contends that likewise, we find that everything that comes into being, whether external or internal, is connected to pleasure, pain, or delusion. We may therefore say that they have a common cause in pleasure, pain, or delusion. Here the cause of the world is shown to consist of three modes (*guṇa*s): whatever is of the nature of pleasure is *sattva*, pain *rajas*, and delusion *tamas*.

The following is an example of how things are individually found to be connected to the three *guṇa*s: Among the wives of Maitra, Padmāvatī makes him happy. What is the reason? With regard to him, *sattva* is the mode that emerges. She makes her co-wives unhappy. Why are they unhappy with her? With regard to them, she makes *rajas* the mode that emerges. But when Caitra, who is infatuated with her, cannot have her, he suffers delusion and grief. Why? With regard to him, she makes *tamas* the mode that emerges. And all things may be explained as like Padmāvatī. Therefore, we can infer that the entire world, which is connected to pleasure, pain, and delusion, has those three as its cause. The *guṇa* triad is called "primordial matter" (*pradhāna*), since the world is set out or made by it. Another explanation of the term *pradhāna* is that it is that into which the world is absorbed at the time of universal dissolution (*pralaya*). Primordial matter is insentient, like clay and gold, and unfolds of its own nature to accomplish the purposes of conscious beings, whether they be enjoyable experiences or ultimate liberation. But it is not set in motion by any agent whatsoever. For Sāṃkhya texts include such statements as "The five sense organs, the five organs of action, the mind, intellect, and ego are triggered by the purposes of the self (*puruṣârtha*), not by any agent."[7]

Śaṅkara: Against this we argue as follows. If the Sāṃkhya position is to be established simply on the strength of the examples presented, then it is sufficient to point out that nowhere in the world is there found something

7 *Sāṃkhya-kārikā* 31.

insentient that generates effects that are capable of satisfying an individual's goals independently, without being directed by a conscious entity. For, in the world, things like houses, palaces, furniture, and parks are found to be made by intelligent craftsmen. As the need arises, they are constructed so that we may gain pleasure and avoid pain.

In the same way, this entire universe consists of external things like earth and the other elements, which facilitate experiences that follow from various actions, and of animate things like the living bodies found in various species, whose arrangement of parts and organs is precisely fixed such that the body can facilitate experiences which follow from various actions. This entire universe is observed to have been fashioned intelligently; a universe so wonderful that it is beyond the conception even of the most imaginative, ingenious craftsmen. How could insentient primordial matter have arranged this, since nothing of the sort is found to occur for rocks, clods of earth, and the like? Orderly arrangement (*racanā*) is found to take a specific form in materials like clay when they are shaped or directed by potters. The philosophical problem facing Sāṃkhya is that primordial matter should also be similarly shaped or directed by an entity other than itself who is conscious.

In addition, there is no rule requiring that we try to understand a root cause only in terms of a feature that stems from the intrinsic function of the material cause, like considering only things like clay when trying to understand a clay pot, and ignoring external factors like the potter.

Vācaspati Miśra: Against this, Śaṅkara says: In addition, there is no rule . . . ascertainment of a natural connection rests on positive and negative correlations.[8] And positive and negative correlations with a conscious factor are absolutely evident, just as it is absolutely not evident that there are such correlations with an unconscious material cause. So enough here with the discussion of what is essential—this is the gist of Śaṅkara's statements.

Put in the contemporary language of fallacies, Śaṅkara is accusing the Sāṃkhya philosophers of something akin to "proof by selected instances." Sāṃkhya's argument by analogy focuses only upon the fact that a wide range of created effects

---

8 Please see pp. 54–55 of this volume for further discussion of this point.

require material causes. It uses this fact as the basis of its argument that the fundamental cause of the universe must be an ultimate material cause. Śaṅkara responds that if we are to take ordinary instances of created things (like clay pots) as our guide, then what's also required are conscious, purposeful craftspersons who make such things in order to satisfy particular needs of individuals (like the desire to hold water for cooking or drinking).

Śaṅkara: Furthermore, it is not true that our understanding contradicts the teachings of the Upaniṣads in any way. Rather, our view is in accordance with the revelations of the Upaniṣads because we assert that the cause of the universe is conscious.

Therefore, for the reason given in this sūtra, **because the world arrangement would be inexplicable**, an insentient cause of the universe is not to be inferred.

The word "**and**" in the sūtra is used in order to allow for the rejection of other Sāṃkhya arguments for insentient primordial matter, since such arguments, like that from *uniformity*, are untenable. For we cannot prove that distinct types of external and internal things are uniform just because they are composed of the triad of pleasure, pain, and delusion. Things like pleasure are considered internal (i.e., mental), whereas objects like sound are not understood to be internal in nature. Furthermore, we think of external things as causing internal events (e.g., music causes the mental state of pleasure). And a single instance of something like an external sound is experienced in peculiar ways as pleasure or something else like pain, because of distinct mental dispositions belonging to different perceivers.

The same reasoning holds concerning the Sāṃkhya argument from the delimited nature of effects. We observe that the production of things like roots or sprouts requires several factors coming together. Likewise we can infer that external and internal things in general require the coming together of several factors, *since they are delimited.* The philosophical problem facing Sāṃkhya here is that the modes *sattva*, *rajas*, and *tamas* should also be preceded by the coming together of several factors, since they are no different in being delimited. In contrast, the causality observed in the case of such things as furniture, which are fashioned in such a way that they are delimited, is that they are preceded by intelligence. Therefore, basing one's thought on there being in place a causal relationship, one cannot think that distinct things—internal as well as external—are preceded by an absence of consciousness.

§ § §

Sūtra 2.2.2. *pravṛtteś ca* |

And because of action, the Sāṃkhya primordial matter cannot be proved.

Śaṅkara: Now let us put aside the world's arrangement and consider action (*pravṛtti*), which Sāṃkhya also gives as a reason to establish that insentient primordial matter is the ultimate cause. Such action is held to be an original disturbance from a natural state of equilibrium, the manifestation of a condition where some of the *guṇas* (*sattva*, *rajas*, and *tamas*) subordinate others.

But action is always directed toward specific effects to be accomplished. And such would not be possible for insentient primordial matter acting spontaneously, just as we observe with clay and chariots. As they are themselves insentient, neither clay nor chariots are found to act in pursuance of specific effects without being directed by conscious beings such as potters or horses respectively. And as a general rule, we reason to what we have not experienced by appeal to what we have experienced. Therefore, also since its creative action would be impossible, an insentient cause of the universe cannot be inferred.

> **Vācaspati Miśra**: In the absence of conscious oversight, a lump of clay does not become predominant and make the potter's wheel, stick, water, and thread subordinate (in order to turn itself into a pot). Therefore (like Sāṃkhya's other provers already considered), action also proves that there is guidance by a conscious being. The Sāṃkhya prover, *since causal efficacy initiates action*,[9] is thus also contradictory, as it establishes the opposite of what they hope to prove.

9 *Sāṃkhya-kārikā* 15.

Objection: We do not find action in mere consciousness (without a body) either.

Śaṅkara: That's true. Nevertheless, what is observed is action on the part of something insentient, for example, a chariot, when it is connected to a conscious being.

> **Vācaspati Miśra**: The Sāṃkhya objector is saying "You Vedāntins find our provers defective and want to establish that a conscious being alone, without depending on anything else, is fit to be the material and efficient cause of the universe. That however is not right, because action on the part of mere consciousness is not found in the case of the things cited as examples."
>
> The Vedāntin tells the Sāṃkhya advocate to first accept that action is caused by a conscious being. Later, the Vedāntin will concentrate on specific ideas belonging to his own theory. Having this intention, Śaṅkara concedes, "That's true." A conscious being acting entirely on its own (without a body) is not observed.

Objection: But even when it is connected to something insentient, we do not find that a conscious being possesses action.

Śaṅkara: Are we sure that this is the right thing to say on the issue? If action is observed in something (e.g., a body or physical object), then does it belong to that very thing? Or, if it is observed in something intimately connected with something else (e.g., a conscious being) does it belong to the latter?

Objection: That in which action is observed is precisely that to which it belongs.

Śaṅkara: So the right thing to say is that it belongs to both, since that is what is observed.

Objection: But a conscious being is not observed to be a sole locus of action the way a chariot is. Rather, the settled true nature of the conscious self is that it is connected to things like the body, which are the loci of action. This situation of a living body is found to be entirely different from, for example, a chariot which on its own is insentient. Just for this reason, furthermore, the materialist Lokāyatikas understand consciousness as well as other properties to belong to the body alone because when a perceivable body exists, consciousness is observed and when there is no perceivable body, it is not observed. Therefore, action does not belong to a conscious being by itself.

At the heart of classical Sāṃkhya is a radical and uncompromising dualism between matter and consciousness. For Sāṃkhya, all activity is within the province of matter and all consciousness is within the province of conscious selves. To motivate this idea, they claim above that the notion of a conscious being acting without a host of physical prerequisites is unheard of. In response, Śaṅkara is trying to think through the way that conscious beings and insentient causal conditions work together to generate action.

Śaṅkara: This is our answer: We Vedāntins do not deny that action found in something insentient belongs to it. Let us assume that it belongs to that alone. We do say, however, that action comes to be *because* of consciousness. When consciousness is present, action occurs, and when consciousness is absent, no action proceeds. For example, even though the change characterized by burning and light is nested in wood and even though the change itself is not directly perceived, it happens only when there is flaming heat, just *because* of the flaming heat. This is because it is observed in conjunction with heat, and never observed in its absence. The reasoning about action and consciousness is similar.

Vācaspati Miśra: First of all, it is not our intention now to prove the existence of an individual embodied self or of a supreme self, as these have already been accepted on the basis of perception, inference, or scriptural testimony. We simply want to assert that they are causes of action. No action is observed on the part of a dead body or a chariot or the like when they are not guided by consciousness and, conversely, action is observed when they are guided. Therefore, through positive and negative correlations, we can be certain that action has a cause in consciousness.

Our position is not, however, that the existence of consciousness *alone* causes action, since this claim would generate unacceptable counterexamples.

Even those who view consciousness as a property of material elements do not dispute the fact that action on the part of things that are not conscious is due to their being guided by conscious beings. So Śaṅkara says below, "The materialists, too . . . "

Śaṅkara: The materialists, too, concede that, by observation, it is only a conscious body that initiates action belonging to insentient things such as chariots. It is not a matter of dispute that an instigator of action would be a conscious being.

Objection: Being an instigator of action is impossible for your conscious self (*ātman*) even when it is connected to a body, etc., because it is incapable of action, as action is opposed to its essence as self-knowledge or awareness at the very least.

Śaṅkara: No, for the situation is like that of a magnet or like color, which, although devoid of action, can instigate action. That is, it is like a magnetized stone that although itself devoid of action instigates action in iron. Or, it is like objects such as colors and so forth that although themselves devoid of action instigate action on the part of the likes of the visual organ. In this way, the Lord (*īśvara*), who, although devoid of action, is omnipresent, the self of everyone, all-knowing and all-powerful, can instigate anything. Thus, it is possible.

Objection: To be an instigator is impossible for the Lord because of his unity; there would be nothing separate from himself to instigate.

Śaṅkara: No. For we have refuted this objection more than once by the (idea of) the power of *māyā* for "names and forms" (i.e., appearance of individuals) made manifest by "spiritual ignorance," *avidyā*. Therefore, it is possible that there be action on the thesis that the all-knowing Lord is the cause, but not, in contrast, on the thesis that the cause is something insentient.

While they may look similar, the arguments advanced under 2.2.1 and 2.2.2 are different in important ways. The first argument is concerned with the arrangement of the world. It contends that arrangement for the sake of achieving certain purposes is possible only when there is conscious direction behind it. Therefore, the Sāṃkhya view that insentient primordial matter creates the world, with no influence of conscious agency, is wrong.

The second argument focuses more generally on the notion that action requires consciousness as a causal condition. Here, Śaṅkara grants for the sake of argument that action itself is located in physical bodies. Nevertheless, such action still requires the influence of consciousness as one cause among others. Therefore, the Sāṃkhya view that insentient primordial matter can act to create the world, without the influence of conscious agency, is also wrong.

As Vācaspati notes, the bulk of the argument so far is not an explicit development of core Vedāntic views as much as the general case that actions and structured arrangements must have consciousness as an aspect of the causal nexus that produces them. But the final portion of Śaṅkara's commentary does begin to delve into essential theological concerns of Non-dual Vedānta. The opponent argues that if the ultimate reality is, as alleged by Non-dualists, unified consciousness, then there would be nothing to create or to make, as there would be nothing separate from God or Brahman in the first place. But Śaṅkara responds with the notion of the world as māyā, *the power of "spiritual ignorance,"* avidyā, *to make manifest our world of "names and form."*

§ § §

Sūtra 2.2.3. *payo-'mbu-vac cet tatra api* |

If it is argued that primordial matter can act, just like milk or water, the reply is that in those cases too there is guidance by a conscious being.

Objection: What you said above may be true but consider this. Milk, which is insentient, comes forth simply of its own accord in order to nourish a calf. Water, which is insentient, flows simply of its own accord in order to benefit the world. So, in the same way, insentient primordial matter is primeval cause, and functions simply of its own accord in order to accomplish people's goals.

Śaṅkara: What you say is not right. In the cases of milk and water, which you cite, we rather infer that activity is guided by a conscious being. For we do not find activity on the part of such things as mere chariots, which are insentient. The chariot example is accepted by both our sides.

> **Vācaspati Miśra**: The objector argues "as there is intrinsic activity in milk and water that is not governed or guided by a conscious being, the *pradhāna* may be conceived in this way too." This is the crux of the doubt. Our response is that we are trying to prove that in those cases the condition "being guided by a conscious being" also applies. To allege that they are counterexamples with respect to the property to be proved would result in the destruction of inference in general. For in every case, this could easily be alleged.

Śaṅkara: Moreover, sacred literature teaches that the Lord (*īśvara*) guides and oversees the entirety of this fluctuating universe, as we find in such verses as (*Bṛhadāraṇyaka Upaniṣad* 3.7.4) "That which stands in the waters, governing the waters from within" and (*Bṛhadāraṇyaka Upaniṣad* 3.8.9) "At the command of that imperishable one, O Gargi, some rivers flow east while others flow in other directions." Therefore, the argument that **primordial matter can act, just like milk or water**, is unsound, since these examples fall within the scope of that which is to be proved.

> *With this last point, Śaṅkara and Vācaspati are arguing that since the Vedāntic view is that God governs the actions of the natural world, it is improper to use things drawn from the natural world as counterexamples to the general claim that structure and change require agency. It is these, along with other created things, that Vedānta is arguing about. To use them as counterexamples would be like appealing to a certain politician's character as evidence to refute the argument that* that very politician is dishonest *when it is the character of* that very politician *that is under dispute.*
>
> *When Vācaspati says that allowing these as counterexamples would undermine all inference, he is pointing out that if it were legitimate to take the objects under*

dispute and use them as counterexamples to an inference, then in principle any inference could be instantly refuted in this way.

Śaṅkara: Furthermore, it could be that the flowing of the milk comes from the affection and desire that the mother, who is conscious, has for the calf. It is by means of the sucking of a calf, who is a conscious being, that milk is drawn out. Nor is even water active independently from everything else, since its flowing is dependent on the slope of the ground and other factors. But dependence on a conscious being is illustrated everywhere.

Objection: Elsewhere in this text (*Brahma-sūtra* 2.1.24) there is the following: "**If you object to the thesis that Brahman is the singular cause of the world, on the grounds that we find agents utilizing a collection of instruments, we say, no, for it is like milk, which changes into curd on its own, without instruments.**"

This sūtra says that Brahman can create the world on its own, without any external instruments. It uses an example similar to that discussed above, milk's changing into curd without the need of external help or assistance. The opponent is citing this sūtra to suggest that even according to Vedānta's own texts, the view advanced under 2.2.3, that insentient matter cannot act on its own, is refuted. But Śaṅkara and Vācaspati Miśra both argue that the two sūtras are operating on different registers. They aren't actually in conflict at all.

Śaṅkara: In that earlier sūtra, the point is to provide an example from our world of everyday experience to show that an effect can come to be of its own accord, independently of external instruments. However, on the other hand, there is the current teaching of dependence on the Lord which is happening everywhere as illustrated by sacred literature—the one view does not repel the other.

Vācaspati Miśra: That (earlier) sūtra was articulated with concern for the naïve perspective from everyday life, not from the perspective transcending it (provided by our current theological inference).

§ § §

Sūtra 2.2.4. *vyatireka-anavasthiteś ca anapekṣatvāt* |

Primordial matter could not unfold on its own, since (i) there would be nothing in that state which is different from it and (ii) it does not depend upon anything else.

Śaṅkara: According to Sāṃkhya philosophers, primordial matter amounts to the three *guṇa*s resting in equilibrium. Outside of that, there is nothing at all external to it abiding in that state upon which its movement or cessation would depend. The conscious individual beings are the only additional item, but are conceived as detached, neither instigating primordial matter nor stopping it from acting. Thus, it is wrong to hold, as do Sāṃkhya philosophers, that independent primordial matter sometimes transforms into the Great (*mahat* = *buddhi*) and other emanations and sometimes does not. In contrast, the Lord can be conceived without contradiction as freely acting and desisting from action (to create the world), owing to his inherent omniscience, omnipotence, and power of *māyā.*

Vācaspati Miśra: It is not acceptable that distinct changes occur by happenstance. In contrast, according to our theological theory, we account for the initiation and cessation of creative action, because they belong to the Lord, who is conscious, possesses cosmic power of *māyā*, and works in accordance with the results of creatures' karma, whether his own reason for creation is divine play, pure spontaneity, or his own diverse nature.

In their account of this sūtra, our commentators stress the point that, as understood by Sāṃkhya, primordial matter has nothing beyond itself to initiate the creative act. As such, why it would ever transform into the world of categories and objects or why it would ever cease such fluctuations is a mystery. On the other hand, if it is accepted that there is a Lord who stands above and controls matter, and who has consciousness, volition, and power, then we at least have an account of why the creation may be initiated or brought to an end.

It is noteworthy that Vācaspati is not committed to any specific account of the Lord's motivations to create. This openness is consistent with what we take to be the core insight of Advaita Vedānta, led by Śaṅkara, that the human powers of conceptualization cannot stretch beyond the creation. An Advaitin is willing to argue up to the limits of human rationality, and then depend upon sacred revelation for further information, or simply refuse to make further claims.

§ § §

Sūtra 2.2.5. *anyatra abhāvāc ca na tṛṇâdi-vat* |

And primordial matter is not spontaneously active in the manner of grass and the like because grass does not change into milk anywhere else than in a cow's stomach.

Objection: Maybe. But consider this. Within a cow's stomach, grass, sprouts, water, and so on change into milk simply of their own nature, independently of any other causal factor. In a similar way, primordial matter will change to assume the form of the Great (*mahat*) and the other emanations. And how, you may ask, do we infer that grass and the like do this independently of another causal factor? It's because no other factor is found. For if we were to discover one, then having procured grass, we would be able to create milk should we desire it. However, we are not able to do so. Therefore, the transformation of grass and the rest is intrinsic. Likewise, primordial matter could also self-transform.

Śaṅkara: To this we reply as follows. If the notion that grass changes intrinsically were acceptable, we would concede that in the same manner, primordial matter changes according to its intrinsic nature. But it is not acceptable, since other causal factors are found. If it be asked why, the answer is given in the sūtra: **because the change of grass into milk does not happen elsewhere than in a cow's stomach**. For it is only when consumed by a cow that things like grass become milk. It doesn't happen when it is left uneaten or is consumed by the likes of a bull. For if this were to occur independently of instrumental factors, then things like grass would become milk in other places, too, and not just when related to a cow's body.

Moreover, it is wrong to hold that when human beings are incapable of creating something according to their own whims, we must conclude that there is no cause for it. For some things are brought about by human beings and others by fate (*daiva*, "the divine"). We could also say that humans, too, are able to produce milk with the appropriate means, after collecting grass. For the milk they want originates on the condition that wanting it, they give the grass they have collected to a cow. And thereafter they get the milk they may be said to have originated. Therefore, it is not the case that we should accept that there is intrinsic change on the part of the primordial matter because of a similarity to grass and so forth.

§ § §

Sūtra 2.2.6. *abhyupagame 'py artha-abhāvāt* |

Even if it were conceded (that it could move spontaneously), primordial matter still would not act on its own because it has no purpose.

Śaṅkara: It has been established now that intrinsic activity cannot occur on the part of primordial matter. But in deference to the belief of you Sāṃkhya philosophers, let us presume that it could act spontaneously, simply by its nature. There is still a defect that would beset your view. And what would that be? That **primordial matter still would not act on its own because it has no purpose**.

First of all, if there were intrinsic activity on the part of primordial matter, such that we should say that the activity does not depend on anything else, then just as there would be no auxiliary cause or condition on which the activity would depend, so too would its purpose also not depend on anything. Thus the Sāṃkhya thesis that primordial matter acts in a way to accomplish people's *ends*—whether enjoyment or liberation—would have to be relinquished.[10] That is, if, as you say, it acts alone and does not depend on any auxiliary at all, then it would also not depend on a purpose either.

If, in spite of this, you say that there is a purpose to primordial matter's activity, then we must examine what it is, whether enjoyment or liberation,

10 See *Sāṃkhya-kārikā* 21 for the claim that creation unfolds in order to serve two major purposes: to allow individuals to experience the world and to allow liberation.

or both. If it is enjoyment, then we ask what kind of enjoyment could there be for a self (*puruṣa*) understood to be a being whose greatness is beyond conception? There is also the difficulty that there would be no liberation (since the purpose of primordial matter would be to generate experiences perpetually). If its purpose is liberation, then since the supreme good would already be accomplished even prior to its activity, creation would be pointless. And there would be no experience of sense objects, sound and the rest.

If both enjoyment and liberation are to be accepted as the goals of primordial matter, the difficulty still remains that since things to be enjoyed are endless, in reality nothing but primordial matter in its unending forms, there could be no liberation (since the goal could never be fulfilled).

Furthermore, its activity could not have cessation of desire as its goal, since neither insentient primordial matter nor the unblemished, undivided conscious self are loci of desire.

If you are worried that the inherent power of seeing (belonging to the self) and the inherent power of creation (belonging to the *pradhāna*) would be pointless so that we must presume that primordial matter has purposeful activity, then you face the difficulty that there could be no liberation. For the power of seeing and the power of creation never go away. Furthermore, *saṃsāra*, the round of birth and rebirth, would never end.

Therefore, the thesis that primordial matter is motivated by the purposes of mankind is wrong.

We have already seen two major attacks on Sāṃkhya's thesis that insentient primordial matter independently creates the world: (i) in our experience, structure is correlated with conscious agency, and (ii) in our experience, action requires consciousness as a causal condition.

In the passage just considered, Śaṅkara, following the sūtras, adds a third major problem to the Sāṃkhya thesis: the notion that primordial matter has an end or telos makes little sense. This is an internal criticism of Sāṃkhya—its own view that pradhāna *is impelled by an end is incompatible with other theses held by the school. While Sāṃkhya holds that* pradhāna *creates without conscious agency, it also claims that the creation is enacted "for the sake of the self's experiencing primordial matter"* (puruṣasya darśanârtham), *and "for the sake of the self's complete liberation"* (puruṣasya kaivalyârtham) (Sāṃkhya-kārikā 21). *These purposes are thought to somehow influence primordial matter to unfold at the time of creation. Our Vedāntins argue that this idea is untenable since primordial matter has no goals of its own and isolated pure selves are utterly desireless. According to Sāṃkhya, a pure self, unconnected to matter, is incapable of thought, desire, or any other propositionally structured mental state. It is simply a locus of awareness. As such, it cannot have any desires antecedent to its entanglement with matter. Therefore, there is nowhere to locate purposiveness or goal-directedness prior to the creation.*

§ § §

Sūtra 2.2.7. *puruṣa-aśma-vad iti cet tathā api |*

If your contention is that a *puruṣa* (pure self) moves primordial matter like a magnet, similar problems remain.

Objection: Maybe. But consider the following examples. A crippled person can see but not move, and a blind person can move but not see. As the crippled person is picked up by the blind person and directs their movement, or a magnet, which cannot move independently, can impel a piece of metal to move, in a similar way, the self impels primordial matter to act. By such examples, we set aside your objections.

Śaṅkara: This too is wrong, as it is not free from flaws. First, in what you have just said you abandon your own asserted thesis. Your core view is that primordial matter is intrinsically active, while the conscious self does not initiate activity. And so, to take up your *new* position, how is it that the conscious self, who is fundamentally indifferent, makes primordial matter act? For, even the crippled person uses speech and physical contact to make the blind man move. Thus, there is no means whatever by which the conscious self can initiate action, since by nature, it is inactive and untouched by the *guṇas*. Nor could it do this in the fashion of a magnet, which works merely by proximity. Since the proximity would always be in place—the conscious self is always "in the vicinity" of matter—initiation of action would always occur. This is the difficulty. A magnet is not, in contrast, always in proximity to the bits of iron whose movement it can cause. When it is close, it functions on its own. Furthermore, its working is conditioned by such factors as its having been wiped clean. Thus, your claim that **a *puruṣa* moves primordial matter like a magnet** remains unproven.

Vācaspati Miśra: The Sāṃkhya advocate argues: "Let us *not* suppose that the initiating factor is the conscious self's purposes nor some inherent purposefulness of the forces (i.e., the awareness-force belonging to the *puruṣa* and the creation-force belonging to primordial matter). Rather, let the conscious self, endowed with awareness-force, initiate action in primordial matter, endowed with creation-force, as a crippled person initiates action on the part of a blind person (on whose shoulders he is riding)." But the view cannot rid itself of defects, as Śaṅkara says, "You abandon your own accepted thesis." Not only would Sāṃkhya here abandon an accepted thesis, but this claim is also inconsistent with their own philosophical framework. Thus, Śaṅkara says "how is it that the conscious self, who is fundamentally indifferent. . . ."

Śaṅkara: In summary, for the reasons that (i) primordial matter is insentient, (ii) the pure conscious self is indifferent, and (iii) there is no third thing that could cause the two to be related, there is no possibility of a relation between primordial matter and the conscious self. Furthermore, considering your thesis that the relation arises through an *affinity* between the two: since this affinity is not subject to destruction, your view faces again the difficulty that liberation would not be possible. And so, just like earlier, you would have to maintain that there is no purpose on the part of primordial matter. In contrast, as conceived by us, the Supreme Self is by its self-supporting intrinsic nature both indifferent to activity and an instigator of activity—hence the superiority of our view to that of Sāṃkhya.

In general, Indian philosophers hold that causal influence involves contact of some kind or other. But magnets are typically cited as an example of action at a distance, through some kind of power (sometimes occult or inscrutable). Here, to say that a puruṣa *may be thought to influence primordial matter like a magnet means that simply by being near primordial matter,* puruṣa *would then affect it the way that a magnet affects nearby iron shavings.*

§ § §

Sūtra 2.2.8. *aṅgitva-anupapatteś ca* |

Furthermore, subordination (of one mode to another) is impossible.

Śaṅkara: And from this it follows that one shouldn't think that primordial matter acts at all. For such would require primordial matter, with its uniform essential nature, to cast away the fundamental balance among the modes (*guṇas*). In that state, the three *guṇas* have intrinsic natures independently of one another. It is unacceptable that one could become subordinate to any of the others, because then they would lose their intrinsic nature. Since (on the Sāṃkhya view) nothing external exists that could agitate them, there would be no creation of "the Great" (*mahat*) or the rest of the items of the Sāṃkhya theory, which are said to be caused by non-equilibrium among the modes.

Vācaspati Miśra: Had the state of primordial matter been immutably eternal (*kūṭastha-nitya*), then no change or deviation could be possible. For accepting that the primordial state could change would lead Sāṃkhya to the undesirable position that the primordial state would be non-eternal. It is rightly said: "The wise accept that the nature or essence (*sva-bhāva*) that never deviates from its original state is eternal." That is why Śaṅkara says, "then, they would lose their intrinsic nature."

An objector may ask: "What if the primordial state is mutably eternal (*pariṇāmi-nitya*)? It has been said: "The eternal is that which undergoes changes while its essence remains the same." In response to this, Śaṅkara responds: "Since nothing external exists . . ." How is it that something that maintained a state of equilibrium for a long time could start changing in the absence of any external factor? And if an independent entity somehow starts changing spontaneously, it is not supposed to maintain equilibrium.

As discussed in our introduction to Sāṃkhya, the notion of creation held by the Sāṃkhya interlocutor is that it begins when some of the three guṇas *abandon their state of equilibrium, with some becoming subordinate and others predominant, churning primordial matter to create the manifest world.*

When Sāṃkhya philosophy claims that primordial matter is eternal, there are two models of eternity available to them: the mutably eternal and the immutably eternal. The former is beginningless and endless although it continues to transform throughout eternity. The latter remains unchangingly the same for eternity. Vācaspati wants to show that both the models fail when applied to the state of primordial matter. If it is immutably eternal, nothing will emerge from it; hence there will be no creation. If is mutably eternal, the times of quiet before or after the creation cannot be explained in the absence of an external factor. For primordial matter is insentient; it needs an external factor to trigger its change. If it somehow starts changing spontaneously, it cannot regain equilibrium in the absence of another factor.

§ § §

Sūtra 2.2.9. *anyathā anumitau ca jña-śakti-viyogāt* |

Moreover, (the defects remain) if you make a different inference, since primordial matter is divorced from the power of consciousness.

Objection: Maybe. But we make a different inference that does not have the defect that you have now brought out. For we do not accept that the modes each have intrinsic natures independently and are unaffected, because there is no evidence to support such a view. Rather, the intrinsic nature of the modes is identified according to the nature of the effect one wants to explain. This is the principle: We conceive of things' intrinsic nature according to our understanding of the effects that they produce. And it is accepted that "Restlessness, instability is a property of the modes."[11] Therefore, even in the state of primordial equilibrium, the modes are capable of entering into disequilibrium. That is how they are.

Śaṅkara: Even so, all the defects mentioned earlier, starting with problems involving "world arrangement," beset your idea of that very state, **since primordial matter is divorced from the power of consciousness**.

11 *Yoga-sūtra-bhāṣya* 3.3.

You could never argue that it has the power of consciousness, since that would contradict your basic position. The notion that there is a unitary conscious being, who is the underlying cause of this world's display of multiplicity, is the result of thinking like a Vedāntin, a proponent of Brahman (and thus you surrender your view).

Although you say the *guṇa*s are capable of entering into disequilibrium, when they are in a state of balance they would never do so, as there would be no reason for it. Or, if they did break up and diverge, they would constantly do so, since there is no difference (between the two possibilities), given the absence of a reason or cause. This is the inevitable difficulty, the defect that remains for your view.

§ § §

Sūtra 2.2.10. *vipratiṣedhāc ca asamañjasam* |

Furthermore, because of inconsistencies, the view is contradictory.

Śaṅkara: Furthermore, different Sāṃkhya thinkers endorse contradictory views. Sometimes they enumerate seven sensory and motor faculties, sometimes eleven. Likewise, sometimes they teach that the creation of the subtle elements flows from the Great (*mahat*), sometimes it is from Ego (*ahaṃkāra*). Similarly, sometimes they describe a triad of mental faculties, sometimes one. It is well known that they contradict Upaniṣadic revelation, which upholds the Lord as cause of the world, as well as the sacred texts that follow revelation's teaching. Here, too, the philosophy of the Sāṃkhyas is **contradictory** (with regard to the teachings of scripture).

In the passage that follows, the Sāṃkhya interlocutor will argue that it is rather Vedānta that is contradictory, because Vedānta's non-dualistic view of reality cannot explain how individuals who suffer can transcend the causes of suffering. Since Sāṃkhya is a dualistic school, with consciousness and matter entirely different entities, they argue that Sāṃkhya has a much easier time making sense of the quest for liberation from suffering. This is a powerful attack, since Vedānta, like many other Indian schools, holds that proper understanding of its philosophy, along with appropriate praxis, terminates in freedom from suffering.

Objection: It is rather the philosophy of the Vedāntins that is utterly **contradictory**, because you do not accept that the subject who suffers is a distinct type of thing from that which causes suffering. For in accepting Brahman as unitary, as both the self of everyone and the cause of all manifestations, you must identify the two qualities, *being the sufferer* and *being the cause of suffering*, as belonging to a unitary self. This precludes you from accepting the two as distinct kinds (whereas such dualism is the hallmark of our view).

And if you think that *being the sufferer* and *being the cause of suffering* both belong to a single self, then the self could never be liberated. Vedāntic texts would thus be wrong in teaching that having the right philosophy quenches the fires of suffering. For a lamp whose nature is to emit heat and light doesn't lose that nature in the act of emitting them. You might portray the self by analogy with water, where disturbances of the sea in the form of waves and foam are simply the ever-arising-and-disappearing modes of the water, which itself is a unified thing. In that case, however, water could never be free of waves and foam.

Furthermore, according to common understanding, a sufferer and the causes of the suffering are different sorts of things. For example, a person seeking something and the object sought are to be characterized as mutually distinct. If the object sought did not differ from the seeker herself, then whatever object would make her a seeker would always remain in her possession. Thus there could be nothing that would make her a seeker. For it takes something that is not possessed to make it possible that there be something that is sought by a seeker.

Similarly, nothing would be sought out as a desired object. If non-dualism were true, then the desired object would already belong to itself. And that does not happen. For there are the two relational words with distinct meanings, "seeker" and "sought." And the relation implied would be between two relata, not a single thing. Therefore, these two, seeker and sought, are distinct realities.

Likewise, that which is not sought and the non-seeker are distinct realities, too. The desirable is something the seeker favors; the undesirable is something the seeker does not favor. A single person becomes related to each in due course. Because that which is desired may become diminished and that which is undesirable expanded, the two are both really undesirable; they are both causes of suffering. In contrast, that which suffers is the conscious self who as a single being becomes related to the two, the sought and the not-sought, in due course. Thus, liberation would not be possible if the two, the sufferer and the causes of suffering, have a single nature. But if they are of different kinds, liberation does come about sometimes, specifically by removing the cause of the conjunction.

Śaṅkara: You are wrong. Because of the self's unity, no relation between sufferer and causes of suffering can be understood to apply. Our view would have the defect you allege if, being unified, the sufferer and the causes of suffering were understood to share mutually the relationship of subject and object. But that is not the case with the self precisely because of its unity. For it is not the case that fire, which exists as a single thing, burns itself or illuminates itself, although its properties of being a source of heat and being a source of light are distinct and changeable.

> **Vācaspati Miśra**: Śaṅkara says, "You are wrong. Because of the self's unity, no relation of sufferer and causes of suffering can be understood to apply." Since their identity would fail to account for the sufferer and the causes of suffering, we accept that at the *level of everyday speech and action* (presupposing *avidyā*, "spiritual ignorance") the sufferer is different from the causes of suffering. Repeatedly we have said that suffering itself is phenomenally, but not transcendentally, real. He further says "Our view would have the defect you allege if, being unified, the sufferer and the causes of suffering were understood to share mutually the relationship of subject and object." Had this been our view, it would have been faulty.

Objection: Is the state of being both the sufferer and cause of suffering not applicable to Brahman, which is unaffected and unified? Where else could being the sufferer and the cause of suffering come from?

Śaṅkara: Do you not see that the embodied self, the person formed by karma, is the sufferer and a cause of suffering as well, its originator (in the sense of generating karma)?

Objection: The fires of suffering belong to the conscious being, not to the insentient body. For if they belonged to the body alone, then they would themselves perish when the body perishes. Thus yogic practice would not be advocated (but rather suicide).

Śaṅkara: Without a body, a conscious being on its own is not found to suffer pain. Furthermore, you too find pain not to be a matter of change or deformation of an isolated conscious being. Nor could it be a result of the body and the conscious being having been mixed together, because that idea would generate unacceptable consequences like impurity attaching to the self, contrary to Sāṃkhya doctrine. Moreover, it is simply not acceptable that pain belongs just to itself. So how, then, do you make sense of the relationship between the sufferer and the causes of suffering?

Objection: The mode of *sattva* (lucidity, intelligence) is the sufferer while that of *rajas* (passion, activity) causes suffering.

Śaṅkara: No. According to you, those two cannot become mixed together with the conscious being. If you say that because of absorption in *sattva*, it is *as if* the conscious being also suffers, then from the ultimate perspective, the conscious being never really suffers, because this is what is meant by your phrase "as if." If you hold that the conscious being does not suffer, then use of the phrase "as if" would not be faulty. For in saying that a footless lizard is *like* a snake, we do not imply that it is poisonous. Nor in saying that a snake is *like* a footless lizard do we imply that it is not poisonous.

And, therefore, what should be accepted is that the relationship between the sufferer and the causes of suffering is the product of spiritual ignorance (*avidyā*), and does not belong to the ultimate perspective. Thus our view, unlike yours, is not vitiated by any defect whatsoever.

Objection: Then your position is that the conscious being is really a sufferer. And it is you who must face the difficulty, now all the more worrisome, that liberation would not be possible, since you would also have to accept that causes of suffering do not cease. On our Sāṃkhya view, in contrast, while the power that generates the relationship between the sufferer and the causes of suffering is eternal, it depends on a conjunction that requires a causal condition. Since the conjunction has a causal condition, there can be cessation of the ignorance that gives rise to it. When that happens, a complete cessation of the conjunction is followed by a complete and final liberation. Thus on our view, unlike yours, liberation *is* possible.

Śaṅkara: Wrong. For you, ignorance amounts to the mode called *tamas* (darkness, inertia), which you say is ceaseless. Moreover, since the *guṇas*' arising and predomination are not regulated, the cessation of the cause of conjunction would have to be unregulated, too. Thus, the supposed separation, too, would be unregulated. For that reason, the Sāṃkhya view cannot avoid the charge that liberation would be impossible.

On our Upaniṣadic view, in contrast, the worry that liberation would be impossible cannot arise, even in a dream. For we find the self to be unified; as a single thing it is not understood to be subject to a subject/object relationship. This accords with what we learn from the revealed teaching that from the ultimate perspective, differences of change and deformation belong to the realm of speech and action alone. In the world of everyday speech and action (*vyavahāra*), relations of sufferer and causes of suffering do of course occur. And to whom? Well, it simply happens to some person or other. Here there is nothing to be urged against us, nor must we give up the idea that suffering occurs.

Vācaspati Miśra: Śaṅkara shows that on our view the theory of liberation makes perfect sense, when he says "On our Upaniṣadic view. . . ." An unblemished face can look different from its reflected image, which appears unclean and dark due to the mirror being unclean. In such a case, the unclean surface of the mirror would be a projected attribute (*upādhi*). The surface of the mirror leads to a mistaken attribution of a distinct image to the face. The face is not really dark-complexioned, nor is the reflection (*pratibimba*) entirely different from the original (*bimba*). A dark complexion is associated with the reflection since it is formed on a dirty mirror. Devadatta is unhappy to see his darkish face (in the mirror).

The moment the projected attribute is wiped clean, Devadatta realizes that the original itself has becomes a reflected image as a mental construction (*kalpanā*), but that his face is fine. His suffering subsides since he knows "My face is not darkish." The living being delimited by spiritual ignorance as its main condition is something like a reflected image of the supreme self. The ordinary self suffers due to its identification with words, ideas, and so on as mentally cognized. As a (metaphysical) truth, no suffering belongs to the supreme self.

Immediate awareness of Brahman (the self) arises due to a mature and intense practice of meditation on the teaching "Thou art That" (*tat tvam asi*), having learned it from scripture and having reflected on it in a mature and intense way. Then, the living being becomes aware of the self's true nature as pure and awakened, and obstacles along with the subconscious dispositions that make them entrenched are all wiped away as an entire mass. There is no more fear of transmigration for such a person. Because that to which it is due (viz., *avidyā*) is no longer a reality, the stump and its roots are pulled up.

But the mode of darkness and ignorance (*tamas*) as conceived by Sāṃkhya is always real and is never destroyed. That is why Śaṅkara says: what we learn from the revealed teaching is that in the ultimate perspective, differences of change and deformation belong to a realm of speech and action alone.

Study Questions

1. While Vedānta is typically focused on systematic explication of the Upaniṣadic teachings, both Śaṅkara and Vācaspati argue that it is within the scope of the school to directly refute their philosophical rivals independently of any appeal to sacred testimony. How do they argue this?
2. How do Śaṅkara and Vācaspati argue that order or structure requires agency? What aspect of Sāṃkhya's philosophy is this meant to refute?

3. Commenting on sūtra 2.2.2, Śaṅkara claims that "action is always directed toward specific effects to be accomplished." How is this principle meant to refute Sāṃkhya? Do you agree with this principle? Why or why not?
4. Sāṃkhya argues against Vedānta's notion that action requires consciousness by stressing the fact that we do not observe action without embodiment or the presence of material bodies of some kind. How do our Vedāntin philosophers respond?
5. How do Śaṅkara and Vācaspati respond to the claim that we find various instances of action without conscious guidance within nature?
6. Provide at least two reasons that Vedāntins claim that primordial matter could never initiate creation on its own, as found in sūtras 2.2.4–7. Why do they think that a conscious God, standing above creation, would solve these problems?
7. Why do Vedāntins find the notion that primordial matter is initiated in order to satisfy human purposes untenable?
8. Explain Sāṃkhya's major counterargument to sūtra 2.2.10, that it is rather Vedānta which has a problem, since, according to its own non-dualism, it cannot properly explain how the suffering individual can seek to end its suffering. Is the Vedāntic response adequate?
9. What do "dualism" and "non-dualism" mean when applied to Sāṃkhya and Vedānta respectively.

Suggestions for Further Reading

Brereton, "The Upanishads" is an erudite and concise introduction to the Upaniṣadic worldview assumed by Śaṅkara and all Vedāntic philosophers. Bryant, "Agency in Sāṃkhya and Yoga" examines the Sāṃkhya notion of a pure self as an unchanging monad devoid of agency. Chemparathy, "The Testimony of the Yuktidīpikā" translates the Sāṃkhya case against God as presented in an important early commentary on the *Sāṃkhya-kārikā*.

Deutsch, *Advaita Vedānta* is a creative exploration of Advaita as a coherent conceptual and phenomenological system. Larson, *Classical Sāṃkhya* is a concise, synoptic study of the version of Sāṃkhya addressed by Saṅkara and Vācaspati in their commentaries, which includes a translation of the *Sāṃkhya-kārikā* as an appendix. Lott, *Vedāntic Approaches to God* is an accessible survey of the conceptions of Brahman held by each major Vedāntic school, helpful in situating Advaita within the larger Vedāntic milieu. Potter, *Encyclopedia of Indian Philosophies, vol. 3* provides extensive introductory material on the historical and conceptual foundations of Advaita Vedānta, along with summaries of major early works and commentaries. Rao, "The Guṇas of Prakṛti According to the Sāṃkhya Philosophy" elucidates and critiques multiple interpretations of the *guṇa*s within Sāṃkhya, as well as questions of how they interact and remain in equilibrium and ways they relate to the manifest world. Thibaut, *The Vedānta Sūtras* is a complete translation of Śaṅkara's commentary on the *Brahma-sūtra.*

Part Two

Vācaspati Miśra's Theistic Argument in His *Nyāya-sūtra* Commentary

Rational Theology in the Nyāya Commentarial Tradition

Vācaspati Miśra's argument for God is taken from his *Nyāya-vārttika-tātpārya-ṭīkā* (*Notes on the Gloss on the Commentary on Nyāya*). Like Vedānta, Nyāya is a Vedic or Hindu tradition of philosophy in that it endorses texts and cultural practices that can be traced back to ancient Vedic culture, broadly construed. The term *nyāya* means a rule or pattern of reasoning. As understood by Nyāya philosophers, it is a method of inquiry that may be called "critical investigation." Finally, as the name of the philosophical school, it is often simply translated as "Logic." Nyāya was famous in classical India for epistemology as well as rigorous defense of various metaphysical positions (external-world realism, the existence of selves as psychological substances, mereological holism, and so on). Like Vedānta, Nyāya reveres Vedic literature, especially the Upaniṣads. But whereas classical Vedānta is exegetical in taking its leads from the Upaniṣads, Nyāya appeals foremost to reason and experience. As the passage below illustrates, scripture is sometimes quoted after a case has been made through inference. When it comes to natural theology, Nyāya is famous within Indian philosophy for various arguments in support of an omniscient, omnipresent world creator, the *īśvara* ("Lord").

The passage translated is Vācaspati Miśra's argument for *īśvara* from his commentary on the "theistic sūtras" of the *Nyāya-sūtra*. The *Nyāya-sūtra* is attributed to a person named Gautama, and scholars estimate the earliest sūtras to have been composed around 100 CE. There are three theistic sūtras:

Sūtra 4.1.19. ***īśvaraḥ kāraṇaṃ puruṣa-karmâphalya-darśanāt* |**
The Lord is the cause, since we find that human action is ineffective.

Sūtra 4.1.20. ***na puruṣa-karmâbhāve phala-aniṣpatteḥ* |**
No, that's wrong. In the absence of human action, effects would not arise.

Sūtra 4.1.21. ***tat-kāritatvād ahetuḥ* |**
That, too, is not a good reason, since it is all actuated by the Lord.

In general, distinct interpretations of sūtras are possible, and debates over the exact meaning of these theistic sūtras occur in both classical commentaries and modern scholarship. Indeed, some classical Nyāya thinkers disagree about whose exact views are being expressed in sūtras 4.1.19 and 4.1.20.[1] But everyone agrees that the *Nyāya-sūtra* is making a case for the best understanding of how an *īśvara* fits within a theory of how the world comes about. The surrounding sūtras are concerned with issues of rebirth, karma, and other causal factors that affect the world's arrangement. In this context, the theistic sūtras argue that the *īśvara* is a causal factor for the emergence of macro objects out of primordial, eternal, indestructible atoms. A crucial issue is the relationship between dispositions made by past human action, called karma, and the influence of God. The sūtras proceed in a dialectical fashion. According to the oldest known commentator, Vātsyāyana (c. 450 CE), the first two sūtras voice competing claims, respectively that, first, the *īśvara* has exclusive power, and, second, that human karma does. The final sūtra synthesizes the two positions and presents the correct view: a person's actions shape the future, particularly his or her own, through the generation of karma, but that is itself overseen and actuated by the Lord. While Vācaspati Miśra has a different reading of the exact argument, he does agree with the conclusion that the Lord oversees the creation directly.

---

1 Bulcke, *The Theism of Nyāya-Vaiśeṣika*, 31–35 presents a summary of classical interpretations. Vattanky, "Aspects of Early Nyāya Theism," argues that the original *Nyāya-sūtras* are clearly theistic, consistent with the early commentarial tradition, while Chattopadhyaya, *Indian Atheism*, argues the opposite. The best overview of modern scholarship is Angot, *Le Nyāya-sūtra, le Nyāya-Bhāṣya*.

It is important to keep in mind that classical authors do not simply explain the sūtras they comment upon. In fact, the commentators' historical importance stems mainly from their innovations. Each tacks on several lines of reflection to the ideas of the final sūtra, 4.1.21.[2] Subsequent philosophers—in classical India and in our own day—find these excursions of greater interest than the somewhat narrow question of the precise demarcation of human action versus divine effort in the making of the world.

Vātsyāyana articulates the basic nature of *īśvara* and only suggests that the Lord might be proved by "cognition" (*buddhi*). The second-oldest known commentator, Uddyotakara (540–600 CE), follows Vātsyāyana's lead on the nature of the creator and in making sense of God according to Nyāya's metaphysical categories. But he is the first Naiyāyika in the extant commentarial chain explicitly to argue for the *īśvara*'s existence.[3]

> Primordial matter, atoms, and karma have to be directed by a conscious agent before they can function, since they are insentient, like an axe. As axes, due to insentience, cut only when directed by an axeman, so too do insentient things, such as primordial nature, atoms, and karma, come to function. Therefore, they too are directed by a conscious agent as a cause. (*Nyāya-vārttika* 4.1.21; trans. Dasti and Phillips, *The Nyāya-sūtra*, 120–21)

Uddyotakara's arguments are of a broadly teleological type, rejecting competing options for an ultimate cause of the world's arrangement, including Sāṃkhya's "primordial matter." His main reason there is that Sāṃkhya's atheistic view fails to include conscious agency within the conception of the world's grounds and thus cannot explain how things could have been arranged as they are. But he also reinterprets the theistic sūtras to include debate with Vedānta, which finds a divine being to be the material cause

2 The entirety of Vātsyāyana and much of Uddyotakara, along with selections of Vācaspati Miśra's commentary, appears in Dasti and Phillips, *The Nyāya-sūtra*, 116–36. Some passages translated there have been emended for clarity or to account for Vācaspati Miśra's framing them according to his specific concerns. We have maintained consistency for the most part, but have made a few improvements due mainly to our focus on Vācaspati Miśra.

3 Within Vaiśeṣika, a "sister school" to Nyāya, Praśastapāda (c. 550) introduces arguments for *īśvara* apparently contemporaneously with Uddyotakara. Chemparathy, "The Īśvara Doctrine of Praśastapāda," provides a summary study.

of the world, whereas Nyāya sees the primordial cause as an efficient or agential cause, as a potter is the agential cause of a pot. Nyāya understands the world to be materially built up out of eternal, indestructible atoms within space. God is an original cause, to be sure, but as an efficient cause the Lord is occupied—from ancient times to this very moment—in world construction, arranging atoms in accord with the specific karma of individuals. Given this theory—and insofar as Nyāya's God also does not interfere with karmic justice—we may say that Nyāya has a limited, "minimalist" theism. Individual Nyāya philosophers may have had more robust religious allegiances,[4] but as Naiyāyikas they argue for a restricted theism as supported by reason.

Vācaspati Miśra (fl. 960 CE) stands as the third major known commentator on the *Nyāya-sūtra*.[5] In the title of his work, *Notes on the Gloss on the Commentary on Nyāya*, the word *Gloss* refers to Uddyotakara's work, and *Commentary* refers to Vātsyāyana's. According to the genre presuppositions of a commentary, we are to understand his primary task as a commentator to be the elucidation of Uddyotakara's or Vātsyāyana's arguments and claims. But he is also an original thinker in his own right, and he goes on long excursions on what appear sometimes to be tangential topics. With the theistic sūtras and prior commentary, he provides a fresh interpretation and a rather original argument in defense of Nyāya's *īśvara* thesis. In fact, his commentary could be divided into two halves. In the first half, he is explaining, developing, and, in some cases, reinterpreting the work of his two great predecessors, along with the sūtras themselves. Then he explicitly marks a transition, taking up the entire question of God in a fresh way, making an argument in his own voice. In so doing, he gives us nothing less than a lesson in logic itself, systematically arguing why his proof is free from a number of logical

4 A number of early Nyāya and Vaiśeṣika philosophers are thought to be affiliated with Śaiva and Pāśupata traditions.

5 Between Uddyotakara and Vācaspati Miśra, other Naiyāyikas made important contributions to Nyāya theism outside the mainstream commentarial chain on the *Nyāya-sūtra*. These thinkers include Aviddhakarṇa (c. 620–700 CE), who is said to have commented upon Vātsyāyana's *Bhāṣya*, but who is now known only through fragments of his work that are preserved within Buddhist critiques; Jayanta Bhaṭṭa (fl. 880–890 CE), who wrote a non-commentarial treatise on the major topics of the *Nyāya-sūtra*; and Bhāsarvajña (c. 950 CE), who composed an independent treatise on Nyāya.

flaws alleged by atheists. Our translation below is of the entire second half, Vācaspati Miśra's own comprehensive case for God.

Vācaspati Miśra's Opponents

While Vātsyāyana lays the foundations for Nyāya's theism and Uddyotakara inaugurates its tradition of systematic arguments for God, it is Vācaspati Miśra who brings Nyāya's rational theology to philosophical maturity in responding to sophisticated challenges that arose after Uddyotakara. From the middle of the first millennium CE to the time of Vācaspati Miśra, Indian philosophy entered a period of heightened logical precision and an expanded lexicon by which inferences could be categorized and critiqued. A pivotal figure in this development is the Buddhist logician Dignāga (480–540 CE). After Dignāga, philosophers in various schools incorporate and respond to his innovations in logic and epistemology, and there is overall increased sensitivity to logical rigor within philosophical disputes. Two philosophers in particular harness developments in logic and epistemology to formulate new ways of attacking Nyāya's theism, the Mīmāṃsaka (Vedic Ritualist) Kumārila (540–600 CE), and Dignāga's Yogācāra Buddhist successor, Dharmakīrti (550–610 CE). The two have markedly different philosophical allegiances, but find commonality in their resistance to theism. Kumārila's refutations of theism are motivated by a desire to protect the status of the Veda as a unique, beginningless guide to moral and religious duty, independent of any author, including God. To this end, he also attacks the notion that the Buddha could be an "all-knowing" authority about religious practice. By competing sources of authority being undermined, the Veda's unique status remains. Dharmakīrti, too, seeks to refute the notion that there could be an omniscient creator God who is a source of religious authority. His rejection of philosophical theism is also in accord with Buddhist metaphysical theses concerning causality in particular. According to Buddhist Yogācāra philosophers, to be real is to enter into causal relations. The interactions result in a new world every moment. An eternal, immutable God could not create anything. "Without being changed, one is incapable of being a cause" (*Pramāṇa-vārttika* 1.23). Several authors develop these criticisms in the centuries before Vācaspati Miśra, including the Mīmāṃsaka Maṇḍana

Miśra (c. 700 CE) and the Buddhists Śāntarakṣita (725–788 CE), Kamalaśila (740–795 CE), and Prajñākaragupta (750–810 CE).

Following Uddyotakara, Vācaspati Miśra interprets the theistic sūtras as rejecting (among other things) a Vedāntic understanding of a divine being as the material cause of the world. But he largely ignores Vedānta when articulating his own philosophical theology in Nyāya. The opponents whom he cites voice the critiques advanced by Kumārila, Dharmakīrti, and their followers. Readers may consult Appendix B for the original formulations of many of the objections considered by Vācaspati Miśra below.

Vācaspati Miśra's Comprehensive Argument for God

From His Commentary on *Nyāya-sūtra* 4.1.21

Vācaspati Miśra: So far we have unpacked the teachings of our revered teachers. But a doubt remains. There are three kinds of things in the universe: (a) those known to have an intelligent maker, such as palaces, watchtowers, gates, and arches; (b) those known not to have an intelligent maker, such as atoms and ether; and (c) those for which having an intelligent maker is in doubt, such as bodies, trees, earth, and mountains. There is doubt about this third group's having an intelligent maker, either because it is something that is yet to be known or because it is disputed, and no knowledge source that would settle the matter has been identified, nor any defeater that would rule out a possible view. And it is false that mere non-perception is enough to refute the thesis of the Lord's existence, as there may be existing things that by nature are imperceptible, like atoms.

And so we argue:

1. Things that are the subject of dispute, like bodies, trees, mountains, and the ocean, have a maker who is knowledgeable about their material causes,
2. since they are produced; alternatively, since their material causes are insentient.

3. Whatever is produced—and whatever has a material cause that is insentient—like a palace, has a maker who is knowledgeable about the material cause.

4. Things that are the subject of dispute, like bodies, trees, mountains, and the ocean, are produced and have insentient material causes.

5. Therefore, they too have a maker who is knowledgeable about their material causes.

The first prover given here, "being produced," is not *unestablished*,[6] since the things in question are composite (and thus produced). Also, they have intermediate size (they are not all-pervasive like ether nor infinitesimal like atoms), and they can be moved, as is the case for pieces of clothing (which are effects made of parts and can be moved).

Furthermore, it would be wrong to hold that this inference is trying to *prove what is already admitted* simply because Buddhists accept that individuals' volition influences the formation of things like the earth and Mīmāṃsakas accept that conscious selves do the same. While both these opponents do indeed believe there is consciousness, what is required here is conscious agency coupled with direct awareness of material causes such as earth atoms and the like. Conversely, if they do in fact admit that there is direct awareness of the material causes, then they admit that there is a Lord! May this be indeed a case of *proving what is already admitted*! Who would not want his own view to be established so easily?

And it is false that the example we give is *lacking the property to be proved.* For things like clothes have the property of being produced by weavers who are directly aware of the material causes upon which they work.

By framing the agency in question as having direct awareness of the material causes, *Vācaspati Miśra is trying to delineate a feature that is present in potters, carpenters, and the like, but that also, when applied to effects like the earth and human bodies, would demand that there be a being with unique cognitive capacities. We may note that with this, he tries to avoid the trilemma advanced by Kumārila and Dharmakīrti as seen in Appendix B.*

---

6 For explanations of *unestablished, prover, inferential subject,* and other logical terms used here, see the Introduction to this volume.

Vācaspati Miśra: For the same reason, our proof does not commit the fallacy of *contradiction*. The fallacy of contradiction would be committed here only if pots, cloth, and the like did not have agents as causes, agents directly aware of the material causes. And our opponents don't contend this anyway.

Objection: Maybe. But there is contradiction, because knowledge sources militate against a specific implication within your proof: as a creator, the Lord would have to be embodied. For example, consider the following bad inference: Snow is fiery, since it is impacted by transformation of straw, grass, and the like. Here, the expectation that there is something fiery hot to the touch is contradicted and defeated by snow's touch that is cold. Similarly, in your inference to God, God's knowledge is said to grasp material causes of the world like earth atoms.[7] But (like every other instance of knowledge that we are aware of) such knowledge would have to be produced by a collection of causes that include a knowing self which is tethered to an inner faculty of attention (*manas*) and has a body. In the absence of any of these, knowledge could not arise. Therefore, your argument is to be rejected. Furthermore, our countercontention is well-established and not defeated by any consideration you have advanced. If the collection of causal factors including a body were not in place, then no knowledge would occur, just as, when heat is absent, there is no fire, since no source of burning would be present.

Vācaspati Miśra: You are wrong. If *x* does not entail *y*, then the absence of *y* does not entail the absence of *x*. If *y* can be counted a cause for every instance of *x* when it is not entailed by *x*, then, hooray, you've done away with reasoning altogether! Your objection would have been on target if the cosmic maker's knowledge of material causes of things like earth were itself an effect. But the Lord's knowledge is eternal (and not an effect). This must be admitted. Therefore, the Lord's being unembodied does not mean that the Lord lacks the knowledge needed to create. Let me repeat, if *x* does not entail *y*, then the absence of *y* does not entail the absence of *x*. If this principle did not hold, then when Maitra does not own a horse, he would also not own a cow.

7 Reading *kṣiti* instead of *kṣipta* (Thakur 564.9).

Furthermore, however many non-eternal instances of knowledge are identified, they would not rule out the possibility of eternal knowledge. For, clouds, which are composed of water vapor, are non-eternal, as is the color that inheres in clouds. But this doesn't entail that the cause of clouds, water atoms, along with their own inherent color, are non-eternal also. Both of our sides accept that something that exists without being caused is eternal. It is wrong to hold that since we find, here and there, that knowledge is accompanied by things like a body, it should be concluded that every instance of knowledge entails the knower's having a body. For entailment is an essential relation. And it requires the absence of "additional conditions," *upādhi*. The entailment that you suggest, namely, that every instance of knowledge correlates with embodiment, depends upon an additional condition, *being produced*. For knowledge that is produced does depend upon peculiar causes such as the subject's having a body. But something eternal does not depend upon causes like that. Eternal knowledge is not refuted by repeated experiences of correlation between *produced knowledge* and *having a body*.

Consider the good inference formally stated as follows, "Sound is non-eternal, since it is produced, like a pot."[8] Someone may try to confute this reasoning by claiming that there is a difference of properties between the thing to be proved and the example: If sound is non-eternal because it is produced—a property shared with a pot—then, wow, just for this reason sound also has color! But if sound doesn't have color because of such similarity, then you can't say it is non-eternal on the same grounds.[9] An objector reasoning in this way would commit the fallacy called *false rejoinder by addition of a property*, and would be wrong. Anyone committing this fallacy is mistaken, as their response would be on the basis of mere similarity that is superficial and irrelevant. If that were allowed, inference would altogether implode, since every single inference could be confuted easily.

---

8 This is a standard example of an inference found in Nyāya (e.g., Vātsyāyana's commentary on *Nyāya-sūtra* 1.1.34). Things like pots are obviously produced and therefore time-bound and impermanent. Sound is also impermanent, since it is also produced.

9 This is a stock example of a specific "false rejoinder" (*jāti*) called "false rejoinder by addition of a property," and is discussed at *Nyāya-sūtra* 5.1.4. False rejoinders are akin to fallacies. Specifically, they are irrelevant considerations put forth by one debater to confute another's inference by a kind of trickery hinging on shared properties. They are defined in *Nyāya-sūtra* 1.2.18. See Dasti and Phillips, *The Nyāya-sūtra*, 195.

Objection: Maybe. But your argument establishes only that the property *being produced* entails *having a maker knowledgeable about the material cause*, as seen in examples like pots, but nothing more than this. You may establish this much only for things like earth. Where do you get the distinct property *having a maker with eternal knowledge that grasps all things*? For it is not found in examples of things produced such as pots.

Vācaspati Miśra: (Consider an analogous way of reasoning that we all accept:) From the property *being an action*, which holds for our perceptual experience of colors and so on, how do we get an inference proving the existence of sense faculties? For we don't find that actions such as cutting prove that there are sense faculties. Rather, they prove the existence of things such as axes. But by force of *being a property of the inferential subject*, the inferential mark, *being an action*, does prove the existence of sense faculties, although, indeed, it is not found to belong to the example. For the fact that perception of color is an action means that it relies on an instrument that is capable of producing perceptual cognition. According to the principle of what's involved in *being a property of the inferential subject*, we are led to eliminate instruments such as axes, which do not have the proper character, and conclude that there are faculties of sight and so on, although they are not directly observed.

The same holds here with the argument for the Lord. If the maker's knowledge were not eternal (uncreated), and did not range over all things, there could not be what there is in fact: the simultaneous production of effects throughout immeasurable and unlimited space at every place and location, effects perceptible and imperceptible in animals and plants and the organic world as a whole and so on, from which we prove that the maker is the Lord.

And such knowledge belonging to the Supreme could not be produced by things that are themselves effects, created bodies and sense faculties like our own. We would have to conjure up yet another Lord to produce such a body that is capable of generating the knowledge in question, and this would entail an unavoidable difficulty, since before that second Lord we would need yet another to create *his* body, ad infinitum. It is better to propose a single, imperceptible being with eternal knowledge than innumerable imperceptible beings.

From this consideration alone, the proposal that there is an eternal body or eternal senses is also rebutted.

By this reasoning, the following objection is set aside:

> It may be that anything that has organized structure has some kind of intelligent cause. But how from this could *a single* cause be proved?[10]

One who wishes to refute the omniscience of the maker could do so if fleshy eyes had the power to perceive atoms as well as witnessing selves along with their karma. But there are no fleshy eyes with such capacity. Therefore, you would have to postulate many beings capable of perceiving such supersensible things who would be very different from us and our kind. It is better, for the sake of simplicity, to posit just one such being.

The objection that initiates the current passage is that all the objects in the reference class that do indeed show correlation between being a product *and* having a conscious maker *are artefacts whose creators are ordinary, embodied, and limited beings like us. There are no God-like makers in our experience. Thus the tie between* being a product *and* having a conscious maker *cannot generate knowledge of a God-like maker without violating the nature of legitimate inference which depends on precise correlations.*

Vācaspati Miśra responds by arguing that inferences as captured in the classical Nyāya syllogism may include an element of what Western philosophers call inference to the best explanation. The procedure relies on what is called pakṣa-dharmatā-balāt, *"from being a property of the inferential subject." This is the principle that specific details about what's inferred may be filled out, as a secondary step, according to what else we know about the subject taken to be the locus of the prover. For example, an anthropologist infers that footprints found in a rock stratum are humanoid on the grounds that the prints have properties that are reliable indicators of human feet. She may then further unpack details of the specific humanoids in question, such as migratory patterns or likely diet, according to what would be required for the creatures to be in a position to leave such traces in the area. This unpacking is based on the footprints* being a property of the inferential subject.

10 This quotation is from Maṇḍana Miśra's *Vidhiviveka* (155), a Mīmāṃsā text which Vācaspati Miśra himself commented upon.

That is to say, it is because they are located in distinct rock strata, with specific features of their own.

When Vācaspati Miśra says that the cosmic maker's knowledge ranges over "the simultaneous production of effects throughout immeasurable and unlimited space at every place and location, effects perceptible and imperceptible in animals and plants and the organic world as a whole," he is making a similar case. His claim is that once we see that human bodies, mountains, and the like are produced by a conscious agent, we think of a maker who is capable of all this. Obviously, no ordinary agent fits the bill. Thus we infer a God-like maker.

Objection: We can explain the arising of effects like bodies and earth merely from the connection between individual selves and atoms, like the fruition of karma (*adṛṣṭa*, "Unseen Force") when it matures. Who needs conscious agency?

Vācaspati Miśra: This should not be alleged. The tie between being produced and having an agent who is directly conscious of the material causes is established naturally, and it is free from "additional conditions."

Objection: Your argument is beset by *deviation*, since we know that (a) without supervision, the mind and senses produce cognition, (b) without guidance, insentient milk flows of its own accord from old to young cow, and (c) without conscious effort, trees flourish in the forest.[11]

Vācaspati Miśra: That is wrong. You cannot use these cases as counterexamples, as they are among the things that we are arguing about in our very proof; they are targeted in our inference as what the dispute is about.

And you cannot simply rule out intelligent agency here because it isn't directly seen, in the way that we deny that a rabbit has a horn on its head. Since the Lord is not fit to be apprehended by ordinary perception, proof by non-perception does not apply here. Further, if one held that non-perception of something that another person is trying to prove were enough to rebut the proof, then inference would be finished! Of course, we accept

11 See Vācaspati Miśra's commentary on *Brahma-sūtra* 2.2.3 (in Part 1 of this book) for a similar objection against Vedāntic theism, which Vācaspati Miśra puts forth on behalf of a Sāṃkhya interlocutor.

the evidence of non-perception regarding something like a rabbit's horn, since such a horn would be in principle perceptible, like the horns of horned animals such as calves.

The objector argues that there are examples of products that come to be without conscious oversight: trees in the forest, milk flowing from cow to calf, and our own cognitive apparatuses generating knowledge without the need for something over and above superintending the productive processes. Vācaspati Miśra's response is to reiterate that his argument is framed to include these cases within the domain of objects targeted. It is just this sort of thing that the inference shows is shaped by the Lord. Thus they can't be legitimately cited as counterexamples without undermining a basic principle of logic. In Western terms, this would be said to be "begging the question" against the theist.

The objector may remain unsatisfied, however, since clearly we do not perceive a conscious being influencing the growth of trees. Shouldn't this non-perception be enough to rule out the thesis that the cases in focus have agential causes in the first place?

Vācaspati Miśra's response is to argue that non-perception is definitive proof that something does not exist only if the thing is ordinarily perceptible. We know that rabbits don't have horns because horns are perceptible and we would perceive them if they were there. Non-perception does not count as evidence against the existence of atoms, in contrast, since atoms are not perceptible. The Lord is not perceptible according to Vācaspati Miśra, since he does not have a body with which our sense faculties could be connected.

Objection: Maybe. But it is false that the simple fact of *being produced* naturally entails *having an intelligent agent.* Rather, it is only a certain kind of *being produced.* When someone notices something whose creation she has not personally witnessed, she still knows that it was crafted if it is something like a pot, whose existence or nonexistence is known to conform to the existence or nonexistence of an intelligent maker. But it does not hold for those things that have the unqualified property of *being produced*, like organic bodies and earth, since these things are not experienced as being associated with makers in the way you propose. Therefore, the general property, *being produced*, is tied to *having an intelligent maker* only when there is an additional condition (*upādhi*) that qualifies it (namely, *being the sort of thing that we have* *experienced as having makers in the past*). There is no natural entailment between the two but only one that requires this additional qualification. Therefore, *being produced* cannot establish your claim. If it could, there would be the unacceptable consequence that one could infer fire merely from the whitish color of smoke—even when the color inheres in lotuses or doves—since it supervenes on the natural entailment between smoke and fire.

Vācaspati Miśra: Here is our answer, which you should think about carefully. Consider the following two options: Does the certain kind of *being produced* that you admit correlate with (a) intelligent agency in general or (b) only with that intelligent agency previously experienced as connected to it? If the first, then yours is our position, precisely what is accepted by us who maintain that things like organic bodies and the earth have an intelligent maker as a cause. For one cannot shamelessly deny the correlation between an effect and its cause. Then, to consider the second option, if this particular kind of *being produced* correlates only with things that have already been directly experienced to have intelligent makers, then people who have not witnessed something's being made would not be able to know it has a maker. Only that very cloth that has been experienced as conforming to the presence or absence of an intelligent maker could be inferred to be the product of intelligent agency, and not some other one in the market.

Objection: Maybe. But then what we should say is that things of *the same kind* are perceived to correlate positively and negatively with having an intelligent maker, even if some specific thing in question is not directly experienced as such. Being of the same kind, it would be a similar case.

Vācaspati Miśra: Come now, this is not a stick by which you can drive us away! Things such as pots, insofar as they are *produced*, correlate positively and negatively with *having a maker with intelligence*. Something else of the same kind, namely, things produced, such as organic bodies and the earth, would be similar, that is, have a maker with intelligence. If you say that only things in the class of pots correlate with an intelligent maker in being produced, then palaces and the like could not be known to have had an intelligent maker by dint of their having been produced. They are not in the same class as pots.

We may accept that something not directly experienced to correlate positively and negatively with having an intelligent maker can be known to have one, but only so long as things of its kind are found to correlate. But now please tell us, how is it that things such as palaces that have been made are thought to have intelligent makers whereas things such as organic bodies and the earth are not? We may assume that in both cases there has been no direct experience of correlations. There is indeed no difference at all with respect to being of the relevant type. Though an anthill is akin to a pot in that it is a transformation of clay, we know that it is not made by a potter, since we do not observe a visible potter. In the case of organic bodies and the earth, the intelligent maker must be understood to be imperceptible.

Objection: Maybe. But it is not the case that *being produced in general* entails having an agent who has direct awareness of the material causes. Rather, being produced *with material causes of the sort we are capable of knowing* is what entails it. And the earth and organic bodies are not these sorts of things. And therefore, since there is no genuine entailment, it has not been proved that they have an intelligent agent.

Vācaspati Miśra: That is wrong. First, through positive and negative correlations, it is established that there is an entailment between *being produced in general* and *having a conscious agent who is knowledgeable about the material causes*. Then, to account for a maker's awareness of their own creation, we must further conceive of an agent whose knowledge is capable of targeting the material causes of the products in question. From this, and since we don't find any additional conditions that are required, there is a natural entailment between being produced and having an intelligent agent. And although we are extending its normal scope, it shouldn't be doubted. If you did, you would be abandoning the very idea of natural entailment.

Objection: Maybe. But the inference you put forth is fallacious, since it is neutralized by counterinferences like the following: "Earth and the rest are *not* brought about by an all-knowing being, since they are objects of knowledge, like a pot." These inferences prove the opposite of what you are trying to prove.

Vācsapati: We respond to this as follows. Is your reasoning meant to refute *being produced by an all-knowing agency*, or *being produced by mere conscious agency*, with the omniscience inferred as an additional step? If the former, then you still accept that earth and company are made by a maker, although not an omniscient maker. This itself would be to abandon a core tenet of your own. And it is not possible anyway, since beings like us, whose knowledge arises after creation, could not create things like earth. Or, if you are trying to refute the latter, the second option, mere conscious agency, your reasoning fails since it doesn't account for the obvious fact that things like pots—your very example—are made by conscious agents!

Objection: Here is another inference: "The Lord does not oversee things like atoms, since the Lord does not have a body, like liberated selves." And another, "The Lord's cognition does not range over all things and is non-eternal, since it is cognition, like ours."

At this point of the discussion, the opponents try a different tactic and instead of merely trying to point out flaws in Nyāya's proof, offer direct counterarguments to nullify the conclusion that the Lord exists or that there could be a Lord who is omniscient or capable of creating the world.

Regarding the example of liberated selves, according to the mainstream Nyāya account, liberation amounts to an individual self becoming untethered from a body and from the internal faculty of attention, the manas. *Vātsyāyana apparently views a liberated self as being in a state of painless stasis, neither acting nor enjoying propositional awareness of any kind, and while some other Nyāya philosophers appear to imagine a richer existence, his view does not appear to be rejected by Uddyotakara or by Vācaspati Miśra. Vācaspati Miśra has an opponent use the idea to argue that an unembodied Lord could not superintend creation; similarly, no liberated self could do so since it would also be bodiless.*

The response below is that since the objector's point presumes the Lord's existence, it cannot be well-formed unless one accepts that existence. Further, since the idea of a Lord includes its having maximal knowledge as well as being the arranger of the world, these properties are packed into the very concept.

Vācaspati Miśra: You are wrong. For either of these inferences to be well-formed, that there is a Lord who has knowledge would have to be accepted!

Neither inference can stand on its own terms, and as such they are not probative. From the start, both inferences are doomed by the very knowledge sources required for them to be advanced. For it is not the case that sacred testimony and inference establish the Lord in abstract without the qualities of (a) *having eternal cognition ranging over all things* and (b) *being the creator of the universe.* Accordingly, it is shown that your two inferences, both of which contradict these claims, are not fit to be asserted.

The Lord's desire and effort should also be understood as being eternal like his knowledge, and they are included within the requirements for creation of the world. This is because knowledge, desire-to-act, and effort are essential characteristics of agency. By establishing one of them, the other two are also established. Therefore, by showing nothing more than that things like earth are produced by an agent, and then filling out our understanding of what such an agent must be like, the Lord is shown to have this character.

Or, let's say for the sake of argument that we have established agency with respect to the items under discussion (earth, etc.), only in a very general sense. Yet by an argument from elimination, an inference in negative form, we can establish a specific understanding of the maker. Here is the inference in negative form.

1. The maker of things like bodies and earth, who has knowledge of their material causes, does not have non-eternal, limited cognition.
2. Because otherwise there would be the unacceptable consequence that the maker of things like bodies and earth would not have knowledge of their material causes.
3. For we do not find that a being with non-eternal, limited cognition could have knowledge of the material causes of earth and organic bodies, just as we humans do not.
4. The maker does have knowledge of the material causes of creation.
5. Therefore, the maker does not have non-eternal, limited cognition.

No agent other than a Lord conceived as having features such as unlimited, eternal knowledge could be the agent of creation which requires direct knowledge of the individual atoms and all the immeasurable individual stores of karma made by and housed in individual selves. This was explained above.

By framing the theistic argument in negative form, Vācaspati Miśra is construing the proof as involving two steps. As given earlier, it was a single argument, where the idea of "God" or "the creator" was unpacked according to the principle of pakṣa-dharmatā-balāt, *"from being a property of the inferential subject." Here, as part of a two-step argument, the first step depends on a common application of inductive generalization to claim that the world is a product requiring a maker of some kind. The second step, then, is an elimination of candidates other than an omniscient being who possesses the appropriate desire and capacity. In other words, a God-like being is the only one that could qualify as the maker of things like earth and karma-affected bodies.*

Vācaspati Miśra: The Lord is capable of overseeing karmic merit and demerit which inhere in other selves due to a connection with them. The operative relationship is indirect. It need not be restricted to the two main types of relationship, conjunction and inherence, but could be inherence-in-the-conjoined-conjunct. Atoms and other primitives have to be in contact with the (all-pervading) Lord. And selves are connected to atoms (their bodies are composed of atoms). Karmic merit and demerit inhere in selves. Alternatively, the relationship could be inherence-in-what-is-conjoined on the part of the Lord and selves, the possibility of a beginningless conjunction being realized.

The Lord acts taking into account karmic merit and demerit and the atoms which have their own essential natures. Atoms are predisposed to initiate their peculiar types of effect, without being affected by merit and demerit. The Lord's action is akin to that of someone who knows how to handle poison, which is predisposed to produce its peculiar effects. By this, the Lord's connection with material causes that are conscious is also explained.

Vācaspati Miśra knows that he has to address the question of how God relates to individual selves and especially to their karmic merit, which must be "read" by him to create bodies and circumstances of birth for them in harmony with their just deserts. Nyāya metaphysics recognizes two major types of relationship: conjunction (saṃyoga) *and inherence* (samavāya). *But both of these seem problematic, since* īśvara *is thought of also as in some way transcendent, untouched by karma whether good or bad. Good and bad karma help to make up an ordinary personality and character but not the Lord's.*

In the current passage, Vācaspati Miśra suggests a nested relationship: inherence-in-the-conjoined-conjunct. *A mother can know a child's fever by kissing its forehead. Here the mother and child's bodies would be related by conjunction, by skin-to-skin contact. She then knows of her child's high temperature because of her feeling of bodily warmth. Warmth is a quality that inheres in the body of the child, which is itself in conjunction with the mother. She thus knows the child's temperature through* inherence-in-the-conjoined-conjunct. *In the case of the Lord's knowledge of individuals' karma, the relation that is proposed by Vācaspati Miśra is connection on the Lord's part with the karma in individual selves by way of contact with selves. The relation proposed seems further displaced in that it occurs through contact with the atoms that make up the bodies that are conjoined with selves who are not liberated. Our theorist is, however, not entirely confident about this, it seems, since he also proposes an alternative which also involves displacement. Such a relationship is presumably meant to capture the distance between the Lord and karma. Otherwise, it would seem that the creator would be stained by karma, contrary to the teaching of scripture and religious sensibility.*

Vācaspati Miśra: *Consciousness* is the prover provided by Uddyotakara, understood through indirect indication. Reasons such as *being produced* should be understood as implied according to context.

Sacred tradition reinforces our argument:

This is the Imperishable, Gargī, on whose order the heaven and earth remain separate.[12]

The one God producing heaven and earth.[13]

He reflected to himself: Let me, who am one, become many. Let me propagate.[14]

12 *Bṛhadāraṇyaka Upaniṣad* 3.8.9.

13 *Ṛg Veda* 10.81.3.

14 *Chāndogya Upaniṣad* 6.2.3.

And so on. And also found in authoritative lore:

> The unknowing creature is not the Lord. Moving away from the self (*ātman*), impelled by the Lord, they go toward happiness or distress, toward heaven or hell.[15]

And the Veda reveals that the Lord's knowledge is eternal, without a cause.

> Without feet or hands, he is swift, he who comprehends. Without eyes, he sees. Without ears, he hears. He knows what is to be known, but no one knows him. They speak of him as the Great One, the Supreme Person.[16]

And so on. These very texts show that the Lord is bodiless.

I have elaborated only what was left out by Uddyotakara, the author of the *Vārttika*, and this is now done.

Study Questions

1. What is Vācaspati Miśra's formal "syllogism" for God's existence?
2. Explain what an objector means when each of the following fallacies is alleged to beset Vācaspati Miśra's proof, and, in summary, how he responds to each allegation: *unestablished*, *proving what is already admitted*, *lacking the property to be proved*, and *contradiction.*
3. What views inform Nyāya's contention that things made of insentient material require a conscious agent to form them?
4. Why does Vācaspati Miśra claim that the Lord's knowledge is eternal and uncaused? What objection is this meant to avoid?
5. In his *Dialogues Concerning Natural Religion*, David Hume argues as follows:

   > If we see a house, Cleanthes, we conclude, with the greatest certainty, that it had an architect or builder because this is precisely that species of effect which we have experienced to proceed

---

15 *Mahābhārata* 3.20.28.
16 *Śvetāśvatara Upaniṣad* 3.19.

from that species of cause. But surely you will not affirm that the universe bears such a resemblance to a house that we can with the same certainty infer a similar cause, or that the analogy is here entire and perfect.

Identify at least two specific instances where Vācaspati Miśra's imagined challengers anticipate Hume's concern here. Does Vācaspati Miśra provide adequate responses?

6. Vācaspati Miśra argues that *being a property of the inferential subject* provides a basis to reason that God has unique properties that are unlike those of makers found within common experience. What is this principle of reasoning, what are other examples, and is it acceptable?

Suggestions for Further Reading

Bhattacaryya, *Studies in Nyāya-Vaiśeṣika Theism* surveys some of the major Nyāya arguments for God in various phases of their historical development. Bilimoria, "Hindu Doubts About God" is a study of anti-theistic arguments within Mīṃāṃsā, focusing on Kumārila. Brown, "The Design Argument in Classical Hindu Thought" examines the design argument in its various incarnations within Indian philosophy, including as expressed by classical theists who were both supporters and detractors of the project of rational theology. This work includes a discussion of colonial misunderstandings of Indian theism vis-à-vis the design argument and modern Indian responses. Bulcke, *The Theism of Nyāya-Vaiśeṣika* is a concise examination of Nyāya's rational theology in its early phase. Chakrabarti, "From the Fabric to the Weaver" frames Nyāya's argument as a sort of template and considers various permutations and possibilities. Chemparathy, *An Indian Rational Theology* is an expert study of Udayana's (c. 975 CE) *Flower Offering of Arguments*, which builds upon the work of Vācaspati Miśra and which some consider the apex of Indian natural theology. Dasti, "Indian Rational Theology: Proof, Justification, and Epistemic Liberality in Nyāya's Argument for God" analyzes Nyāya's argument from design in the context of epistemological justification and the nature of inference as a source of knowledge. Dasti, "Theism in

Asian Philosophy" is a summary of the major philosophical themes and schools that are concerned with theism in classical India, looking at both revealed and rational theism as well as their critics. Dasti and Phillips, *The Nyāya-sūtra* is an accessible and philosophically oriented select translation of the *Nyāya-sūtra* along with early commentaries. Chapter 6 focuses on the "theistic sūtras" and arguments for God. Hayes, " Principled Atheism in the Buddhist Scholastic Tradition" is a study of the roots of Indian Buddhist opposition to theism and some of its core arguments. Jackson, "Dharmakīrti's Refutation of Theism" presents Dharmakīrti's anti-theistic arguments, with historical contextualization and select translations. Chapter 2 of Moriyama, *Omniscience and Religious Authority* examines refutations of the notion of an omniscient creator God by Buddhists and Mīmāṃsakas, with some responses by Nyāya thinkers. Patil, *Against a Hindu God* is a philosophically sophisticated study of one of the last major Buddhist critics of Nyāya's argument for God, which engages directly with Vācaspati Miśra's argument. Potter, *Encyclopedia of Indian Philosophies, vol. 2* studies the historical and conceptual foundations of Nyāya, along with summaries of major early works and commentaries.

Appendix A

Śaṅkara, Philosopher and Theist

The introduction at the beginning of this book sketches the life and philosophy of Śaṅkara. There background and context are presented, first the ideas of the original Vedānta of the early Upaniṣads and the *Bhagavad-gītā*—in particular the concept of Brahman—then the philosophical school of Vedānta as an interlocking system of propositions put together in the *Brahma-sūtra* and elaborated in the commentaries of Śaṅkara and others. All that is laid out historically in the manner of an encyclopedia. Now, in contrast, we present a polemical essay aimed not at broadening the understanding of Śaṅkara's problem space and intellectual inheritance but at dispelling two interpretations of the great Advaitin that unfortunately appear to be have become deeply rooted, especially among academics: one, that Śaṅkara was no philosopher presenting arguments appealing to reason but rather exclusively a scripturalist, dogmatically asserting a particular reading of "scripture," *śruti* ("revelation," the revealed "word"), which for him would be certain early Upaniṣads; and, two, that his metaphysics is an illusionism, asserting that all world appearance is *māyā*, "illusion." No, Śaṅkara is a philosopher and a theist.

The portion of Śaṅkara's *Brahma-sūtra-bhāṣya* translated and elucidated in these pages shows a philosophical mind at work such that not much supplementary argument is needed to combat the overly scripturalist interpretation, although combat it further we will.[1] However, the illusionism is a

1 Kapstein, "Interpreting Indian Philosophy" has a section entitled, "Was Śaṅkara a Philosopher?" (23–25) and answers the question in the negative. "In short, for Śaṅkara, soteriology trumps philosophy" (24). But that could be said of several great classical philosophers, including Naiyāyikas as well as great Buddhist thinkers, all who see philosophical reasoning as aiding a spiritual quest. There were also astute anti-intellectualists who saw the two pursuits as opposed but who, like Nāgārjuna, were great dialecticians. We should not be too finicky about the semantic range of

different matter, and its prominence has given the Advaitin the reputation of an atheist. This has become a very commonly made mistake.[2] And once we see how the illusionism characterization distorts Śaṅkara's metaphysics, we may adjust our lens and view his use of the idea of *māyā*, "illusion," as an image standing in for what is truly central in his teaching, which is people's "spiritual ignorance," *avidyā*. Then the further position seems right on track that there should be from that ignorant perspective a certain intellectual indeterminability of the Absolute in its relation to the world, *anirvacanīya*, "it cannot be explained," so goes our argument. Appreciation of the philosophical centrality of this notion of *anirvacanīya* should, in turn, help to clarify the roles of reason and revelation in Śaṅkara's teaching.

In other words, by showing how this concert of ideas—*māyā*, *avidyā*, and "inexplicability"—has been wrongly construed as a cosmic illusionism with little place for a "Lord," *īśvara*, we will establish that Śaṅkara is hardly atheist and is rightly viewed as a staunch upholder of a full-bodied, personalistic theism (the Lord as the original teacher as well as source of the world *both* materially *and* instrumentally), as is consistently taught in the *Brahma-sūtra*. We contend that the Advaitin should be recognized as a theistic philosopher, rationally defending the existence and nature of *īśvara* as taught in the Upaniṣads, and in particular as essential to the right way to think about Brahman, the Absolute, "God," in relation to the world, although we should keep in mind that all teachings of philosophy and of scripture are from the point of view of a fundamental "ignorance," *avidyā*. The right view is that "the Lord" is the source and the fashioner of our universe, which is hardly an illusion. And so we begin with the concept of *māyā*. In line with our focus on natural theology, Śaṅkara's theodicy and reflection on the question of why there is a world at all are presented in a set of extended quotations—a passage comprised of commentary on *Brahma-sūtra* 2.1.33–37—which is meant to supplement, as a defense of theism in the face of injustice and evil, his positive position on the existence of God. The passage also shows the importance of the idea of inexplicability to the right way of connecting the dots of his metaphysics.

---

the word "philosophy." Was Thomas Aquinas not a philosopher because he honored the Bible? Maimonides? Ibn Sinā?

2 Wainwright, "Concepts of God," for example, articulates the widespread interpretation.

Much classical Indian philosophy is written in the style of an implicit dialogue, not so much novelistically, with characters depicted in conversation, but with a wrong view presented first and then an answer given afterwards in response. The wrong view that is presented first in an opponent's voice is intended to seem pretty much right, on the face of it, until the truly right view is spelled out by the author in his own voice, refuting the opponent's prima facie position. But it is also a requirement of the genre to show how the opponent has been seduced into error, so that we all can see how not to go wrong. Here that final task, concerning the error of the illusionist interpretation of Śaṅkara, is pretty straightforward and easy, since it involves the primary persona of our author, which is indeed not that of a philosopher but that of a compassionate "spiritual preceptor," a guru. Śaṅkara's language of practical advice has been misinterpreted as asserting a position about the cosmos as a whole.

The practice of meditation and yoga aimed at self-discovery is Śaṅkara's central advice to his readers. And he sees this as *the* message of the Upaniṣads and the *Gītā*, and, we say, not without grounds. Or at least that this is *a* message is uncontroversial: the *Gītā* famously proclaims that *along with* a yoga of knowledge and meditation there can be a yoga of action and another of devotion. With the former, the idea is that works can be done while acting in a spirit of sacrifice and offering, and the latter has to do with a sense of loving God. Śaṅkara's stress, however, is on "spiritual knowledge," *vidyā*, which, to take up just the contrast with the *Gītā*'s yoga of works, he sees as the premier path. This the path of meditation he sees as antithetical to action undertaken by agents such as us—and he seems to have in mind in particular the religious actions promoted by ritualists called Mīmāṃsakas—agents such as us who desire certain outcomes or are pursuing certain goals. Not religious practices and rituals and sacrifices—no matter that they are prescribed in the Veda (according to some)—but quietness, inaction coupled with attentiveness, sitting down and watching one's own thought and emotion, and trying to make it silent so that one may attend to one's own witnessing consciousness itself. One disengages from worldly concerns and all everyday identity to focus on consciousness itself. Any impulse to action is, at least at first and presumably for most of a long period after commencing a meditation practice, a distraction. A desire or even a thought of a high social value has the effect of pulling one back into thinking about what's needed to accomplish something wanted, whether trivial (Is the door to the fridge shut?) or momentous (an important political rally).

Consciousness is naturally "self-illumining," *svayam-prakāśamāna*, but most of us need to make an effort not to ruminate, to still the stream of thought and feeling, so that the natural ineliminable ability of each of us as a "self," *ātman*, to know our own consciousness itself can shine forth and dominate our awareness as opposed to remaining a background condition making possible customary patterns of speech and action.

This quietism and its intellectual underpinnings in Śaṅkara—who again and again points to the possibility of a radical change of consciousness and no mere change of intellectually formulated opinion—are responsible for the common characterization of his philosophy as an illusionism: the change is said to be so great that we will see our former states in comparison as practically illusory. Of course, this message is, broadly considered, nothing new in Śaṅkara's mileau; it is similar to the Buddha's message as well as that of the yoga of, especially, certain Upaniṣads. The very epithet *buddha* means "awakened," implicitly comparing non-*nirvāṇa* experience to a dream. Our point is that to stress that there is a radical change of consciousness available to us and to use illusion as a way to stress the enormity of the change is not to say that the world positively is, in fact, illusory.[3] Brahman as the material and instrumental cause of the world who indwells as our very self and consciousness does not create unrealities except in the sense that to identify with anything within the finite world of "name and form," *nāma-rūpa*, is to dwell in spiritual ignorance. And it would be much better, Śaṅkara insists, to live in spiritual knowledge.

"Spiritual ignorance," *avidyā*, is Śaṅkara's primary way of characterizing our unenlightened state. By this he does not mean that we intellectually hold the wrong views but that we are distracted away from noticing the true

---

3 For a prominent example of the mistake, representative and not rare, see the bottom-line characterization of Śaṅkara's worldview in Mayeda's oft-quoted *A Thousand Teachings*: "Thus the Vedānta in the *Brahma-sūtra*, which may be characterized as a realistic monism, was transformed into an illusionistic monism, which regards everything but *Brahman* as unreal" (14). Similarly, Pande's carefully researched study *Life and Thought of Śaṅkarācārya*, although on target along many lines of interpretation, has this summary statement concerning Śaṅkara's metaphysics: "It follows that *Brahman* can be the cause of the world only in the sense of projecting an illusion" (193).

nature of ourselves. To become intellectually a Vedāntin is not the solution, not the way to have *vidyā*, "spiritual knowledge"—that's the message of Gautama, by the way, the founder of the rival school of Nyāya, the legendary author of the *Nyāya-sūtra*. No, the Vedāntic message is captured by lines from the *Kenôpaniṣad* (and many others), e.g., verse 1.5: "That which is not expressed by words but whereby words are expressed, know that to be Brahman, not that which is worshipped here in this world." Śaṅkara glosses the "whereby" (*yena*) as "[by Brahman], by the light of consciousness" (*caitanya-jyotiṣā*) (*Ten Principal Upanishads with Śāṅkara-bhāṣya*, 22), stressing not only that the Absolute cannot be known intellectually but also that consciousness, the "self," *ātman*—our own consciousness and self—makes possible all speech and action. Śaṅkara is no Buddhist. Brahman as the Lord is responsible for our world, and is as our own self and consciousness the very condition for the possibility of the whole range of everyday experience as well as the "living liberation," *jīvan-mukti*, of spiritual knowledge, *vidyā*.

Now our minds do demand an intellectual picture. Pursuit even of enlightenment—purportedly a state of consciousness free from pursuits—requires an understanding of ourselves in relation to Brahman even though the goal is that Brahman be known in a non-intellectual way. And for that, to our great good fortune, we have revelation supported by reason.[4] Interpretation of the Veda, to include the Upaniṣads, their most important part, their "fulfillment," *anta* (as in *veda-anta* = *vedānta*), is complicated. Readings conflict, even just with respect to the Upaniṣads. This is one place where reason comes to our aid. Another is argument forged independently of scripture, as illustrated by our selection in Part 1. Both scripture and philosophy operate within *avidyā*: "Perception and the other sources of knowledge and Vedic texts (i.e., Upaniṣads) make pronouncements within the province of *avidyā*, 'spiritual ignorance'" (Śaṅkara, *Brahma-sūtra-bhāṣya*, Introduction). If Śaṅkara is not a philosopher because of his *avidyā* teaching, neither is he a scripturalist.

The founder of Vedānta as a school, the peerless (legendary) Bādarāyaṇa, distills in the *Brahma-sūtra* the teachings of the Upaniṣads and fashions a

---

4 The issue of the respective roles of reason and scripture in the formulation of the Advaita worldview has been addressed by several scholars, notably Wilhelm Halbfass (*Studies in Kumārila and Śaṅkara*), K. S. Murty (*Reason and Revelation in Advaita Vedānta*), and Eliot Deutsch (*Advaita Vedānta*).

system of interlocking claims and rational refutations of competing systems. Śaṅkara says about Bādarāyaṇa's accomplishment, "This systematic study is commenced in order to determine the meaning of Vedāntic statements." Arguments in support of the truth of those statements and refutations of contrary positions are, as he also says in our own selection, "not to establish or refute some thesis by argument alone, like the study of reasoning (*tarka-śāstra*)." The passage continues: "Nevertheless, those who would explain Vedāntic statements should disprove Sāṃkhya and similar views which stand opposed to the right view. It is for this purpose that a new section is commenced. Achieving certainty about the content of Vedānta is for the sake of having the right view. One's own position becomes firm through that certainty" (Part 1 above, at sūtra 2.2.1).

And just what is "one's own position" here? Well, the *Brahma-sūtra* opens by declaring in its second sūtra—after sūtra 1.1.1, "Then, therefore, enquiry into Brahman," *atha ato brahma-jijñāsā*—that, sūtra 1.1.2, "Brahman is that from whom this world proceeds and so on" *janmâdy asya yataḥ*. Śaṅkara explains that the "and so on" in the sūtra is there to include maintenance and dissolution. And throughout his *Brahma-sūtra-bhāṣya*—and in all his works—we are told that it is by the power of the omniscient, all-pervasive "Lord," *īśvara*, who is the world creator, sustainer, and destroyer, that Brahman is "that from whom this world proceeds." How can this be interpreted as atheism?

To have the theistic view of the world—the Vedāntic view of the world—that is articulated and defended by Bādarāyaṇa is not to have spiritual knowledge, *vidyā*. The Brahman to be known in immediate experience, *brahma-sākṣātkāra*, is transcendent to thought, is intellectually unknowable. And that includes how the world looks from Brahman's perspective. This is not to say that there is no relation of Brahman to the world or that the world is an illusion from that perspective, but rather to insist on the spiritual unknowability of Brahman by the mind. Scripture supplemented by reasoning gives us the *best* view against the backdrop of Brahman's strict inexplicability, but we should not pretend that the view delivers intellectual knowledge like that we have of everyday facts and practices. Intellectual knowledge can be extremely important, however. Proper understanding of an Upaniṣadic statement such as *"tat tvam asi,"* "Thou art That," can trigger self-realization.

Indeed, the concept we have of Brahman, of "God," has lots of content beyond the thesis that all thought and conceptualization belongs to our realm of *avidyā*. Advaita is not a negative theology, despite its inexplicability thesis. It takes very seriously, seriously as philosophy, what is learned from the Upaniṣads and Vedāntic *sāstra*, in particular, that Brahman is existent and real, *sat*, conscious, *cit*, and bliss, *ānanda*, as well as all-pervasive and the cause of the world, both materially and instrumentally. The neo-Vedāntic attitude is that the declarations of the Upaniṣads providing the foundations for Vedāntic philosophy are themselves founded on mystical experience, i.e., enlightenment, non-intellectual experience of Brahman. But this is controversial and possibly anachronistic concerning Śaṅkara's view of the authority of scripture and the role of reason in hermeneutics, although there are indeed, as many have pointed out, suggestions of a kind of "mystic empiricism" in the corpus of the great Advaitin.[5] The Veda is not eternal in his view, in flat rejection of the mainstream Mīmāṃsaka position (and Mīmāṃsakas are generally counted in Hinduism the experts for Vedic exegesis). But the Veda does have a self-authenticating validity, not depending on agency, not even the Lord's—in line with the *apauruṣeya* doctrine of Mīmāṃsā, in effect, that the perfection of Veda puts it beyond all agency, which by nature is subject to error and flaws. And when Śaṅkara talks about the Veda, he typically means Upaniṣads. And the Upaniṣads he relies on do tell us a lot about Brahman intellectually, and this, in turn, is supposed to help our spiritual practice and disidentification with things that are subject to change and decay, as our self, we are told, is not.

To be more precise on this delicate issue of Upaniṣadic authority, briefly let us rehearse our Vedāntin's cosmology as we find it in his commentaries. Cosmologically, the Veda is beginningless (*anādi*), according to Śaṅkara. Therefore, it is not a product. This implies that it does not have an original author. But at the time of a world dissolution (*pralaya*), it merges with *īśvara*. Then at the time of a new round of creation (*sarga*), the Lord, who emerges first, makes the "Divine Seed" come forth simply by meditating on the "Word," that is to say, meditating on Veda as *veda-saṃskāra*, as embedded in a "mental disposition" that lies latent during a period of dissolution. Thus,

5 See Deutsch, *Advaita Vedānta*, 81–83; Rambachan, *Accomplishing the Accomplished*, 56–61; and Ram-Prasad, *Advaita Metaphysics and Epistemology*, 6–7, among others.

at first Veda is, strictly speaking, *avyakta*, "unmanifest." The physical Vedas have to be reproduced.[6] The Veda is not eternal since it merges with the Lord and reemerges. It is eternal as a stream, but non-eternal as an individual. It reemerges from the Lord. Thus it is *īśvara-praṇīta*, "brought forth by the Lord." Most importantly, the source of Vedic authority is the fact that the all-perfect Lord recomposes it. No faulty human could do that.[7] Is this not a position we could expect in a full-bodied theism?

As spelled out in the *Brahma-sūtra*, the Vedāntic worldview is not without conceptual knots, like, perhaps, all systems of philosophy (consider modern materialism's "mind-body problem"). Questions about whether Brahman "transmogrifies" in becoming the material world or "self-manifests," along with similarly vexing issues, occupy hundreds of Sanskrit texts in subschools of Vedānta to include further divisions of Advaita. We do not pretend in this essay to unravel every knot in the Vedānta of the *Brahma-sūtra* or in the Advaita system in particular, though we do have something to say at the end about the right way to understand the *advaita* epithet. Nevertheless, a full-bodied theism requires a *theodicy*, an explanation of why things are not as pleasant as we might expect given a compassionate Lord (for example, we might expect "the best of all possible worlds," in the famous phrase of Leibniz). In this spirit, we present a few rather long quotations from Śaṅkara's *Commentary on the Brahma-sūtra*, in which he addresses the issue of theodicy as well as why there is any world at all. The quotations comprise most of a passage that illustrates both the full-bodiedness of Śaṅkara's theism and the often misinterpreted thesis (according to us) of the indeterminability of Brahman. Thus our central contention that Śaṅkara's worldview is no illusionism but a theism is again shown to be textually grounded.

The *Brahma-sutra* passage we will look at here is in fact the text that immediately precedes our selection in Part 1, where Śaṅkara refutes the Sāṃkhya

6 *Bṛhadāraṇyakôpaniṣat* 1.2.4–5: "The self desired 'I should have another self.' So he meditates (and that self comes forth). . . . with that self he brought forth the world, whatever exists: the *Ṛg*, *Sāman*, and *Yājur Veda*, meters, rituals, humans, domesticated beasts." Śaṅkara's comments stress that the Lord's meditation brings out the Veda (*Ten Principal Upanishads with Śāṅkara-bhāṣya*, 619).

7 Precisely speaking, the physical Vedas count among recreated entities including, as Śaṅkara says, "The Vedic verses, prayers, songs, and hymns to include mantras such as the Gāyatrī and so on." *Śāṅkara-bhāṣya* on *Bṛhadāraṇyakôpaniṣat* 1.2.5 (*Ten Principal Upanishads with Śāṅkara-bhāṣya*, 620).

view of the world's arrangement. First, at *Brahma-sūtra* 2.1.33 we have an answer to the objection that the world could not have been created by an *īśvara* because creation is an action and an action by a person requires a motive connected to an idea of something to be accomplished, something desired. Śaṅkara writes:

> Like activities on the part of a prince or minister who has no compelling desire, activities undertaken in playgrounds just for sport (*līlā*) without a particular motive, and like inhalation and exhalation of breath as activities that can occur on their own just from their own nature without regard to any exterior motive, so the creative activity of the Lord we may suppose to come about as nothing but play, sport (*līlā*), just naturally without depending upon any exterior motive whatsoever. For it is false that the Lord has some motive or purpose that is to be discerned either by reason or revelation. Nor is it implausible that the Lord's creative activity is simply a matter of the Lord's nature. Although the universe appears to us to be so intelligently arranged as to require prodigious effort of a very weighty sort, to the Supreme Lord it would all be like mere play, because the Lord's power is immeasurable. Admittedly, in our experience a subtle motive might be detected even in play. Still, no motive whatsoever can be discerned with regard to the Lord's creative action; we know as much from scriptural revelations about those whose "desires are all satisfied." Nor should it be thought that the Lord is not active. Nor that the action is like that of a madman. Scriptural stories there are about creation that say the creative Lord is all-knowing. Moreover, it should not be forgotten that all that we cognize, including from scripture, is limited to that formulable in everyday speech which is a matter of (as the Upaniṣads say) "name and form" (*nāma-rūpa*) conditioned by *avidyā*, "spiritual ignorance," and, furthermore, that the primary intent of the teaching about *avidyā* is that we get the right idea about the self and Brahman.

And so the best intellectual view for us who do not pretend to know precisely how the world looks to the Indeterminable is that the creator easily has the power and knowledge to bring forth this incredible world arrangement. The question is, then, why there is not much less pain and suffering and a much more even distribution of pleasure and happiness than what we see out there in our real but often very unpleasant circumstances. To this question, there is an answer in the next sūtra, *Brahma-sūtra* 2.1.34. Again, Śaṅkara:

> . . . the objection is that no *īśvara* could be the cause of the universe because of the difficulty of **inequality and cruelty** (as the sūtra says) as *īśvara*-perpetrated if it were so. The Lord would be conceived as making some beings—for example, gods and goddesses—exceedingly happy, knowing pleasures in the extreme, while the lot of others—for example, animals—is to have pain in the extreme. And although human beings and the like have pleasures and pains of intermediate varieties, the Lord's creation is such that it is lacking equality of distribution in their having them. Thus the Lord appears to be a particular individual with his or her own personal proclivities, likes and dislikes. The problem here is that the purported teaching of scripture and sacred lore (*śruti* and *smṛti*) would have to be wrong about the Lord's having a nature of purity and other attributes (compassion and so on). Similarly, there is a problem about cruelty abhorred even by the wicked being terribly bad if due to a "Lord." Therefore, so the objection goes, no *īśvara* is the cause of the universe because of the problems of **inequality and cruelty**.
>
> To this, we respond as follows. Inequality and cruelty do not problematize the way we understand the Lord. How so? Because of (as the sūtra says in its later portion) **dependence**. That is, if the Lord alone were responsible for this uneven creation, then the charges of inequality and cruelty would be flaws devastating our position. However, there is no creation without dependence. For the *īśvara* fashions this uneven creation depending on something else. What, you may ask, could that be? Righteousness and unrighteousness, *dharma* and *adharma*, we answer, which, we say, the Lord respects, taking them into consideration in creating. Therefore, it is no fault for which the Lord is to blame in there being this uneven creation that depends on the *dharma* and *adharma* of emergent creatures.
>
> Now the *īśvara* is to be viewed as somewhat like Parjanya, the giver of rain. For as Parjanya is a shared causal factor for the emergence of rice, wheat, and so on while unique capacities are also causal factors

> had just by the seeds of this and that species of plant, so the Lord is a shared cause for the emergence of gods, humans, and so on while the unevenness among these kinds is due to different karma belonging to this and that individual. The distinct karma is a causal factor. So because the Lord fashions in accordance with karma, that is to say, because there is such dependence, our concept of an *īśvara* is not vitiated by the reality of what appears to be inequality and cruelty. There are scriptural statements (*śruti*) to this effect . . . , and also teachings of sacred memory (*smṛti*) that declare that the Lord's favor and its lack depend on the particular karma of creatures, as is said (*Gītā* 4.11, Kṛṣṇa speaking as the Lord), "As they approach me, so do I receive them to my love" and similar statements.

Then we have at *Brahma-sūtra* 2.1.35, the next sūtra, a question about the very first "emergence" (*sarga*, "creation"). Before there was any good and bad karma created by individuals in a previous round, before the cosmic dissolution that preceded a new round of emergence, that is, before there were any good and bad karma-making choices and karmic dispositions said to lie latent (like the "seed Veda") during the dissolution, it does not seem possible for the Lord to have been mindful of any moral deserts in creating and fashioning the manifest universe in a new round. In other words, what about the absolute beginning, before there was any good or bad karma for the Lord to depend upon? Śaṅkara writes:

> An objection is raised that there would be no karma to be depended upon on account of which the creation might have become uneven, because there would be no distinction to be discerned of deeds good and bad prior to the *first* creation. The objection finds support in a scriptural passage, to wit, "The existent alone, my dear, was this in the beginning, one, without a second" (*Chāndogyôpaniṣat* 6.2.1). For karma is acquired at a time after creation. It presupposes diversity of individual bodies and company. And if it is said that the diversity of individual bodies and company depends on karma, circular reasoning is the vitiator. Therefore, we have to say that the Lord could act while considering karma only after a distribution of distinct effects. Because there could be no karma to account for diversity before such a

distribution, the original creation would have to be nothing but equal (in the distribution of pleasures and pains, happiness and suffering).

There is no flaw here, no real difficulty. The objection is rejected since the world of transmigration is (as the sūtra says at the end) **without a beginning**. The objection would be right if transmigration had a beginning. But transmigration has no beginning: like seed and sprout, karma causes and is caused. Thus the idea of the Lord's proceeding to act in creation is not contradicted by the unevenness of the emergent world.

So, how is it established that transmigration is beginningless? We are given the answer in the next sūtra.

Thus Śaṅkara finds a natural order to the sūtras in this stretch of the treatise. There are only two more sūtras until the end of a major division of the *Brahma-sūtra* and the beginning of the passage we have presented above.

Sūtra 2.136. It is rationally a good explanation, and it is found.

Śaṅkara: **It is rationally a good explanation**, that is, the beginninglessness of the transmigratory world recommends itself to reason. For, if it had a beginning, the difficulty would be that the transmigratory world's coming to be would make no sense and, further, that even the liberated might by chance come to be bound again within transmigratory existence. And we would have to live with the unfortunate consequence that what happens would be uncaused, as there would be nothing to account for the uneven distribution of pleasure and pain and like matters.

That it would be no *īśvara* that would bring about such inequality has, furthermore, already been said. We may add that *avidyā*, "spiritual ignorance," could not by itself cause the inequality, since it is uniform. However, *avidyā* could be said to be a factor in bringing about the inequality if it were considered dependent on karma embedding mental dispositions made by obstacles (to liberation) like passion (*rāga*). Furthermore, no living body would be formed in the way it is if there were no karma, while without a living body no karma would be formed. Indeed, there *would* be a circularity predicament, if we assumed a beginning. But if there is beginninglessness, then by the logic of seed and sprout it would all be explicable, **rationally a**

good explanation, such that no vitiation of our view of the Lord's creative action would occur.

The sūtra also says, **and it is found**. The doctrine of the beginninglessness of transmigratory existence is found in both scripture and sacred lore. . . . (*Gītā* 15.3:) "(The extent of the tree of transmigratory existence) is not experienced as such here in this life. It has no end, and it has no beginning. Its permanence is established." This is a verse from sacred lore where the doctrine is found of the beginninglessness of transmigratory existence. And in the Purāṇas as well, it is asserted that past and future *kalpa*s are innumerable.

Sūtra 2.1.37. And because all the properties (needed for creation) are rationally explained (in viewing Brahman as the Lord).

Śaṅkara: Having shown that it is a Vedic teaching (i.e., a Vedāntic teaching), the teaching, namely, that a conscious Brahman is the cause of the universe as well as its material, our esteemed teacher Bādarāyaṇa proceeded to defend the view against failings alleged by others such as the radical differences found in the manifest world. Now about to begin a new section with a new topic—which will be refutations of the positive positions advanced by others in opposition to this view—he summarizes with the current sūtra the main topic of the prior section. This is the topic of why his, and our, own view should be accepted (to wit, that it is taught by the Upaniṣads and withstands rational scrutiny). Given that the view being accepted is that Brahman is the cause of the world, all the properties needed to be that cause are to be rationally endorsed in line with the thesis—to quote our sacred inheritance—"All-knowing, all-powerful, endowed with the great power of delimitation (*mahā-māyā*) is Brahman." Thus is this our Upaniṣadic philosophy beyond reproach.

Our intent in presenting this extended passage from Śaṅkara's *Brahma-sūtra-bhāṣya* is not to put it up for scrutiny—though of course scrutiny is something good—but further to show that Śaṅkara should be considered a theist. There are varieties of theism. Śaṅkara's is not a social doctrine. God does not command us to do good works so much as to discover our true self.

However, making good karma by good works such as charity can be instrumental to having a reincarnation in a body and personality that makes it comparatively easy to achieve enlightenment. And so although it is not his emphasis, there is a social and ethical dimension to his teaching. Śaṅkara's effort counts as philosophical since he has a great sense of coherence, even if his principal goal is to encourage us to take up a yogic path. The linchpin holding together the system is the idea of the intellectual inexplicability of our everyday awareness and identity as it looks from Brahman's perspective. The three translators of this volume have different opinions about the philosophical defensibility of the conception. Does it invite paradox? Is it violated by the very constructions of Upaniṣadic content made by Śaṅkara? Does a person at least have to believe more in order to be motivated to take up a yogic path, which requires sacrifice and commitment? And the path advocated by Śaṅkara and company (*śama-dama-dayâdi-yukta*, "an aspirant should be calm, controlled, and compassionate") would appear to presuppose a more solid connection between the two states than his peculiar psychological dualism supposes. We have individually different thoughts about these matters. Doubtless, others have and will have other estimations. What this essay is stressing is simply that many moderns have been misled by "*māyā*" (!) into missing the centrality of the notion of *avidyā*, "spiritual ignorance," which, should be seen as the basis for both the *māyā* image and its philosophical significance, which is the strict intellectual inexplicability of the enlightened state where Brahman is said to be known immediately, not through words.

In an effort to achieve systematic coherence, the notion of *anirvacanīyatva* is central, as many of Śaṅkara's followers realized. So, in closing, let us say briefly a further word about what Śaṅkara teaches as the surest connection between ourselves as we think of ourselves in everyday life and the enlightened state considered to be a state of non-intellectual knowledge of self and Brahman. This is the Advaita doctrine of consciousness, or of a certain kind of consciousness, a "state" consciousness, not a "consciousness-of," except, perhaps, a consciousness of itself, that is, self-consciousness that is "self-illumining," *svayam-prakāśamāna*. This seems to be the original meaning of the epithet "*advaita*," which, then, more basically than its metaphysical renderings, would be "non-dual" *awareness*. And there is an interesting connection between this idea and the thesis of inexplicability, a connection, we think, that gives Śaṅkara's worldview a certain strength to withstand criticism as well as a certain flexibility.

Self-illumining consciousness is a radically internalist notion. Excepting itself, there is no access to it, nor does it relate to anything other than itself. It is accessible, so to say, only from the inside. Self-illumining consciousness is self-contained, non-relational. So it cannot be explained, *anirvacanīya*. An explanation would purport to find a tie between explanandum and explanans. Self-illumining consciousness can neither be explained nor can it explain anything. From an epistemic perspective, self-illumining consciousness is self-authenticating and, unlike other conscious states and material phenomena, has, we repeat, exclusive access to itself. Thus only it has the right to pronounce on itself. (And then about itself it says nothing.)

As is readily admitted by Śaṅkara and other Advaitins, there is mystery in the transition from other-illumination to self-consciousness in the Advaita sense. That is, we can see the inexplicability thesis from another angle: how self-illumining consciousness is related to the world display is not intellectually determinable, although a kind of theism, Śaṅkara says, as we have seen, is the best theory. More precisely, Śaṅkara does not deny that this consciousness somehow connects with the body and the physical world. There doubtless is a relation, but it is impossible for us to elaborate. There is an uncloseable gap, not between matter and consciousness, but between our thought about the one and about the other. An explanation would be like an unwanted disturbance violating self-illumining consciousness's self-absorbed trance. Thus are we treated to a kind of Advaita "mysterianism" on par with the materialist mysterianism that holds that while everything is material we are constitutionally incapable of understanding how mind reduces to matter. Again, self-illumining consciousness may well not be unconnected to material states; it is nevertheless not connected in a way that can be determined in thought (*anirvacanīya*). Trying to conceptualize the self-illumining self would be like trying to determine at the same instant the position and momentum of an electron. Self-illumining consciousness is inaccessible to representation and all third-person point of view. Talk of it is non-literal, meant to direct a person in herself to the experience.

The mysterianism at the center of Advaita philosophy provides flexibility. Theism, Śaṅkara argues, is the best view, since it is advanced by scripture and supported by reason. Nevertheless, since there is such a radical break between the enlightened state and the everyday person in the everyday world, Advaita in its teaching about the self seems compatible with practically any view of nature.[8] This is underscored by the success of Advaita in various neo-Vedānta theories which rather easily find Advaita to be compatible with science. And although we take Bādarāyaṇa and Śaṅkara to be genuine metaphysicians, their view also resonates with modern skepticism about metaphysics precursed by Vedāntic anti-intellectualism. Indeed, the eleventh-century Advaitin Śrīharṣa, following the lead of the refutations found in the *Brahma-sūtra* as explained by Śaṅkara, is relentless in his attacks on metaphysics, refuting especially the Nyāya theory that would explain definitively a self's relation to the world.

Finally, let us say one more time that we are not purporting to unravel every knot in the Advaita worldview in this essay, but rather to promote a shift of hermeneutic focus. Śaṅkara's theism is central to his understanding of the world. To speak of him as atheistic or averse to theism would be as mistaken as to speak of him as anti-Vedic. In addition, to emphasize the centrality of the doctrine of *avidyā* should also help, we think, to gauge Advaita's strength as a consciousness-centered philosophy.

---

8 At *Śāṅkara-bhāṣya* on *BS* 1.4.14 (*Brahma-sūtra-bhāṣya*, 319–20), the Advaitin says that the objection to Vedānta that the Upaniṣads teach different doctrines of creation misses the point of the passages that do indeed refer to Brahman as the cause of the world. The point, he says, is to assert Brahman as the cause, not to give details of how it happens. Śaṅkara plainly admits that there are different Upaniṣadic accounts of how it happens, but in all cases Brahman is said to be the original cause, he stresses.

Appendix B

Selections from Kumārila's and Dharmakīrti's Critiques of Nyāya's Natural Theology

The following passages are from the *Śloka-vārttika* by Kumārila (c. 540–600 CE), a major philosopher within the Mīmāṃsā school, and the *Pramāṇa-vārttika* by Dharmakīrti (c. 550–610 CE), who is commonly recognized as the greatest exponent of Buddhist Yogācāra philosophy. Each thinker provides systemic critiques of Nyāya's theistic argument, voicing objections that were elaborated and expanded by their followers. Buddhist commentators on Dharmakīrti say that the primary targets of his criticisms are the Nyāya philosophers Aviddhakarṇa and Uddyotakara, both of whom lived a few centuries before Vācaspati.[1] Kumārila's presentation of the Nyāya argument indicates that he has Aviddhakarṇa's version in mind. Dharmakīrti and Kumārila were contemporaries, and questions of their chronological influence are controversial. Krasser, "Dharmakīrti's and Kumārila's Refutations of the Existence of God," however, makes a good case that Dharmakīrti was here influenced by Kumārila.

Kumārila's and Dharmakīrti's overall allegiances in philosophy and religion are quite different, and in fundamental ways their views stand in opposition. Kumārila's Mīmāṃsā is arguably the most conservative Vedic school of thought, and Dharmakīrti's Yogācāra, like most Buddhism, is both philosophically and socially revolutionary. Their arguments nevertheless have several common elements. Each of their critiques is part of larger programs to undermine the idea that a God-like being is a possibility. The criticisms translated below are supplemented by other challenges presented

1 Marks, "Playfighting" provides a helpful study of Aviddhakarṇa as presented in Buddhist sources.

against the possibility of an omniscient creator of the universe (see the bibliography).

One way to understand both Kumārila's and Dharmakīrti's criticisms is that they advance a trilemma, each option or "horn" based upon the type of agency that Naiyāyikas are trying to prove. If Nyāya wants to prove simply that some kind of agency in general helps construct the world, this would commit the fallacy of *proving what is already accepted*, since Mīmāṃsakas and Buddhists accept that individuals' karma helps to shape all future occurrences in the universe. If Nyāya holds rather that the agency involved is akin to that of craftspersons like potters, this would commit the fallacy of being *unestablished*, because effects like human bodies or the earth are radically different from pots or palaces; or it would be *contradictory*, since at best it would establish limited, embodied agents like us, something contradictory to the goal of the proof. Finally, if Nyāya holds that the agency in question is God-like, this would commit the fallacy of the example's *lacking the property to be proved*, since God-like agency is not observed in artefacts like pots. In addition to this trilemma, each of the two anti-theists focuses on problems of inductive extrapolation from ordinary makers to a unique God-like creator of the world.

Vācaspati has all of these critiques in mind as he articulates his proof for God in the *Nyāya-sūtras* (in Part 2 of this volume), and his formulation of key elements within the argument is meant to avoid these pitfalls.

Kumārila, *Śloka-vārttika*, *Sambandha-apekṣa-parihāra*, 74–83a

74 We have a reply to the following argument: "Bodies, like houses, have a distinct arrangement of parts, and their creation is therefore superintended by a conscious being."

75 If what "superintendence" (*adhiṣṭhā*) amounts to is simply being a causal factor, the argument would commit the fallacy of *proving what is already admitted*. It is already accepted that the actions (*karma*) of living beings influence all production.

76 If you instead suppose that superintendence requires desire, the fallacy remains, since actions presuppose desire. If you suggest that the superintendence in this case is special in that the creation arises immediately from the desire, there would be no supporting examples.

77 Furthermore, the prover in your argument would *deviate* with respect to something like the Lord's own body. It too would also have to be created, since it is a body, like ours.

78 You may deny that this is a problem, claiming, "The Lord's body is also brought about through the Lord's superintendence." This is wrong. An unembodied self cannot superintend anything's creation. Consider the example of liberated selves (which are both bodiless and inactive).

79 If you hold that the creative superintendence for things like pots is simply that of potters, then it is not the Lord who oversees their creation. Or, if you hold that for pots, too, the superintendence belongs to the Lord, then the example in your inference *lacks the property to be proved.*

80 And if you take the example as commonly understood, the consequence would be that your prover would be *contradictory*. You could only establish the superintendence of impermanent beings (potters, carpenters, etc.) who are not God-like.

81 If you imagine that the creative action is unlike that of potters (in that it is not facilitated by physical contact), then how could something insentient decide to submit to God's will?

82 Therefore, there could be no original impetus for atoms, etc., to conform to a conscious, creative desire. And if the material origins of things were (instead) an unsullied Person (i.e., Brahman as theistically conceived), the world should have no imperfections.

83a And because moral merit (*dharma*) and demerit would still depend on that Person, afflictions cannot be explained (as simply the results of individuals' bad karma).

As traditionally interpreted, the second half of verse 82 marks a transition in Kumārila's treatise, where he begins to criticize Vedānta and other systems and not just Nyāya's proof. The line and the first half of the next verse bring up the theistic problem of evil and suggest that a standard Indian answer, appeal to karma, does not work.

Dharmakīrti, *Pramāṇa-vārttika*, 2.10–16

2.10 The provers cited by our opponents, *activity after a period of rest, having a distinct structure,* and *acting with a purpose*, each commit the fallacies of *proving what is already admitted*, being *unestablished*, and *doubt about the legitimacy of the example.*

2.11 It is well known that features like *having a distinct structure* correlate positively and negatively with a certain sort of superintendence. That much is correct and fit to be inferred.

2.12 It is not correct, however, to infer something for one set of objects simply because a similar word is used for a different type of thing. That would be like inferring fire merely because one sees something with a pale whitish color (like a dove, which has the same color as smoke).

2.13 Otherwise, we could infer that an anthill is made by a potter on the grounds that certain modifications of clay, like pots, are made by potters.

2.14 (And my criticism does not commit the following fallacy:) When something about an effect is used as a prover because of its connection with the property to be proved, the fallacy of *counterbalancing according to the effect* (*kārya-sama*) occurs if an objector alleges a distinction which is nothing but a superficial difference between the cited example and the effect serving as the prover.

The Nyāya and the Buddhist epistemological traditions both recognize a type of fallacy called "false rejoinder" (jāti).[2] *False rejoinders are attempts to confute a good argument by pointing to false equivalencies or misleading similarities.* Counterbalancing according to the effect *(*kārya-sama*) is interpreted in various ways by early Nyāya and Buddhist authorities,*[3] *but as understood by Dharmakīrti, it is the fallacy of trying to undermine an inference by pointing out a superficial difference between an effect being used as a prover and an effect cited as a token instance of inductive support. Dharmakīrti claims that he is not committing this fallacy by arguing that considered as an effect, something like a pot is radically different from the effects targeted by Nyāya's proof, earth and the like. Despite the appeal, Vācaspati expressly cites this definition by Dharmakīrti while commenting on* kārya-sama *(under* Nyāya-sūtra *5.1.37), and he insists that according to the very standards of the Buddhist epistemologists, Dharmakīrti does commit the fallacy when he criticizes Nyāya's theistic argument.*

2.15 It is wrong to try to prove that something of one type (G) exists on the grounds that the same word is used for it as for something well-attested, but of a different type (F). That would be like trying to prove that speech has horns since it, like cows, is referred to by the word *go*.

The Sanskrit word go *usually means "cow" but is sometimes used to mean "speech." Dharmakīrti is accusing the Nyāya proof of equivocation. In his view, things like pots, used in Nyāya as examples of effects, are so unlike the earth, living bodies, and so on, which are targeted as the subject of the proof, that the word "effect" really means something different in the two cases.*

2.16 Do not all words have referents? It would seem so, since the meaning of any word depends on the intention of the speaker who uses it. But if an object could be proved simply by the use of a word, then anyone could prove anything.

---

2 Matilal, *The Character of Logic in India*, 60–80.

3 Watanabe, "Dharmakīrti on False Rejoinders."

Bibliography

Angot, Michel, ed., trans., and introduction. *Le Nyāya-sūtra de Gautama Akṣapāda, le Nyāya-Bhāṣya d'Akṣapāda Pakṣilasvāmin: l'Art de Conduire la Pensée en Inde Ancienne*. Paris: Les Belles Lettres, 2009.

Bhattacaryya, Gopikamohan. *Studies in Nyāya-Vaiśeṣika Theism*. Calcutta: Sanskrit College, 1961.

Bilimoria, Purushottama. "Hindu Doubts About God: Toward a Mīmāṁsā Deconstruction." *International Philosophical Quarterly* 30 (1990): 481–99.

Brereton, Joel. "The Upanishads." In *Approaches to the Asian Classics*, eds. W. T. DeBary and I. Bloom, pp. 115–35. New York: Columbia University Press, 1990.

Brown, Mackenzie. "The Design Argument in Classical Hindu Thought." *International Journal of Hindu Studies* 12, no. 2 (2009): 103–51.

Bryant, Edwin. "Agency in Sāṃkhya and Yoga: The Unchangability of the Eternal." In *Free Will, Agency and Selfhood in Indian Philosophy*, eds. M. Dasti and E. Bryant, pp. 16–40. Oxford University Press, 2014.

Bulcke, C. *The Theism of Nyāya-Vaiśeṣika: Its Origin and Early Development*. Delhi: Motilal Banarsidass, 1968.

Chakrabarti, Arindam. "From the Fabric to the Weaver." In *Indian Philosophy of Religion*, ed. Roy W. Perrett, pp. 21–34. Studies in Philosophy and Religion, Vol. 13. Dordrecht: Kluwer Academic Publishers, 1989.

Chattopadhyaya, Debiprasad. *Indian Atheism: A Marxist Analysis*. Calcutta: Manisha, 1969.

Chemparathy, George. *An Indian Rational Theology*. Vienna: Indologische Institut der Universität Wien, 1972.

Chemparathy, George. "The Īśvara Doctrine of Praśastapāda." *Vishveshvaranand Indological Journal* 6 (1968): 65–87.

Chemparathy, George. "The Testimony of the Yuktidīpikā concerning the Īśvara doctrine of the Pāśupatas and Vaiśeṣikas." *Wiener Zeitschrift für die Kunde Süd- und Ostasiens und Archiv für indische Philosophie* (1965): 119–46.

Dasti, Matthew R. "Indian Rational Theology: Proof, Justification, and Epistemic Liberality in Nyāya's Argument for God." *Asian Philosophy* 21, no. 1 (2011): 1–21.

Dasti, Matthew R. "Theism in Asian Philosophy." In *The Routledge Companion to Theism*, eds. C. Taliaferro, V. Harrison, and S. Goetz, pp. 23–37. New York: Routledge, 2016.

Dasti, Matthew and Stephen Phillips. *The Nyāya-sūtra: Selections with Early Commentaries.* Cambridge: Hackett Publishing, 2017.

Deutsch, Eliot. *Advaita Vedānta: A Philosophical Reconstruction.* Honolulu: East-West Center Press, 1973.

Dharmakīrti. *Pramāṇavārttika, with the Commentary* "Vṛtti" *of Acharya Manorathanandin*, ed. Swami Dwarikadas Shastri. Varanasi: Bauddha Bharati, 1968.

Dharmakīrti. *Pramāṇavārttika-kārikā*, ed. Yusho Miyasaka. *Acta Indologica* 2 (1971/2): 1–206.

Ganeri, Jonardon, ed. *The Oxford Handbook of Indian Philosophy*. New York: Oxford University Press, 2017.

Gautama. *Nyāya-sūtra*, ed. Anantalal Thakur. *Gautamīyanyāyadarśana with Bhāṣya of Vātsyāyana*. Nyāyacaturgranthikā, vol. 1. New Delhi: Indian Council of Philosophical Research, 1997.

Halbfass, Wilhelm. *Studies in Kumārila and Śaṅkara*. Reinbek: Verlag für Orientalistische Fachpublikationen, 1983.

Hayes, Richard. "Principled Atheism in the Buddhist Scholastic Tradition." *Journal of Indian Philosophy* 16 (1988): 5–28.

Jackson, Roger. "Dharmakīrti's Refutation of Theism." *Philosophy East and West* 36, no. 4 (1986): 315–48.

Kapstein, Matthew. "Interpreting Indian Philosophy: Three Parables." In *The Oxford Handbook of Indian Philosophy*, ed. J. Ganeri, pp. 15–31. New York: Oxford University Press, 2017.

Krasser, Helmut. "Dharmakīrti's and Kumārila's Refutations of the Existence of God: A Consideration of Their Chronological Order." In *Dharmakīrti's Thought and Its Impact on Indian and Tibetan Philosophy* (Proceedings of the Third International Dharmakīrti Conference, Hiroshima, Nov. 4–6, 1997), ed. Shoryu Katsura, pp. 215–23. Vienna: Verlag der Österreichischen Akademie der Wissenschaften, 1999.

Kumārila Bhaṭṭa. *Ślokavārttika of Śrī Kumārila Bhaṭṭa, with the Commentary Nyāyaratnākara of Śrī Pārthasārathi Miśra*, ed. Swami Dwarikadas Shastri. Varanasi: Tara Publications, 1978.

Larson, Gerald. *Classical Sāṃkhya*. Delhi: Motilal Banarsidass, 1979.

Lott, Eric. *Vedāntic Approaches to God*. London: MacMillan, 1980.

Maṇḍana Miśra. *Vidhiviveka of Śrī Maṇḍana Miśra with the* Nyāyakaṇikā *of Vācaspati Miśra*, ed. Dr. Mahaprabhu lal Goswami. Varanasi: Tara Publications, 1978.

Marks, James Michael. "Playfighting: Encountering Aviddhakarṇa and Bhāvivikta in Śāntarakṣita's *Tattvasaṃgraha* and Kamalaśīla's *Pañjikā*." PhD dissertation. University of California, Berkeley, 2019.

Matilal, Bimal K. *The Character of Logic in India.* Albany: State University of New York Press, 1998.

Mayeda, Senyaku. *A Thousand Teachings: The* Upadeśasāhasrī *of Śaṅkara*. Albany: State University of New York Press, 1992.

Moriyama, Shinya. *Omniscience and Religious Authority. A Study on Prajñākaragupta's* Pramāṇavārttikālaṅkārabhāṣya *ad* Pramāṇavārttika *II 8–10 and 29–33.* Leipziger Studien zur Kultur und Geschichte Süd- und Zentralasiens 4. Zurich and Berlin: LIT Verlag, 2014.

Murty, K. S. *Reason and Revelation in Advaita Vedānta*. Delhi: Motilal Banarsidass, 1974.

Newman, John Henry. *Fifteen Sermons Preached Before the University of Oxford Between A.D. 1826 and 1843*, 3rd ed. Notre Dame, Indiana: University of Notre Dame Press, 1997.

Nicholson, Andrew J. "Hindu Disproofs of God: Refuting Vedāntic Theism in the Sāṃkhya Sūtra." In *The Oxford Handbook of Indian Philosophy*, ed. J. Ganeri, pp. 598–619. New York: Oxford University Press, 2017.

Pande, Govind Chandra. *Life and Thought of Śaṅkarācārya*. Delhi: Motilal Banarsidass, 1994.

Patañjali. *The Yoga Sūtras of Patañjali*, ed. James Haughton Woods. Mineola: Dover Publications, 2003.

Patil, Parimal G. *Against a Hindu God: Buddhist Philosophy of Religion in India*. New York: Columbia University Press, 2009.

Phillips, Stephen. "Seeing from the Other's Point of View: Countering the Schismatic Interpretation of Vācaspati Miśra." In the *APA Newsletter on Asian and Asian-American Philosophers and Philosophies* 14, no. 2 (2015): 4–8.

Potter, Karl. *Encyclopedia of Indian Philosophies, vol. 2. Nyāya-Vaiśeṣika*. Delhi: Motilal Banarsidass, 1977.

Potter, Karl. *Encyclopedia of Indian Philosophies, vol. 3. Advaita Vedānta up to Śaṅkara and His Pupils.* Delhi: Motilal Banarsidass, 1981.

Rambachan, Anantanand. *Accomplishing the Accomplished: The Vedas as a Source of Valid Knowledge in Śaṅkara*. Honolulu: University of Hawaii Press, 1991.

Ram-Prasad, Chakravarthi. *Advaita Metaphysics and Epistemology*. London: RoutledgeCurzon, 2002.

Rao, K. B. Ramakrishna. "The Guṇas of Prakṛti According to the Sāṃkhya Philosophy." *Philosophy East and West* 13, no. 1 (1963): 61–71.

Śaṅkara. *Brahma-sūtra-bhāṣya*, ed. J. L. Shastri. With the *Bhāmatī* commentary by Vācaspati Misra. Delhi: Motilal Banarsidass, 1980.

Śaṅkara, *Ten Principal Upanishads with Śāṅkara-bhāṣya*. Śrīśaṅkarācāryagranthāvalī ("Works of Śaṅkara"), vol 1. Delhi: Motilal Banarsidass: 1964.

Thibaut, Georg. *The Vedānta Sūtras: With Commentary by Śaṅkara*. New York: Dover, 1962.

Thibaut, Georg. *The Vedānta Sūtras: With Commentary by Rāmānuja*. Fairford: Echo Library, 2006.

Udayana. *Nyāyakusumāñjali*, trans. N. S. Dravid. New Delhi: Indian Council of Philosophical Research, 1996.

Uddyotakara. *Nyāya-vārttika*, ed. Anantalal Thakur. *Nyāyabhāṣyavārttika*. Nyāyacaturgranthikā, vol. 2. New Delhi: Indian Council of Philosophical Research, 1997.

Vācaspati Miśra. *Bhāmatī (Commentary on Śaṅkara's Brahma-sūtra-bhāṣya)*. See Śaṅkara, *Brahma-sūtra-bhāṣya*. Translation (first four sūtras): S. S. Suryanarayana Sastri and C. Kunhan Raja. *The Bhāmatī: Catussūtrī*. Madras: Theosophical Publishing House, 1933.

Vācaspati Miśra. *Nyāya-vārttika-tātparya-ṭīkā*, ed. Anantalal Thakur. *Nyāyavārttikatātparyaṭīkā* of Vācaspatimiśra. New Delhi: Indian Council of Philosophical Research, 1996.

Vācaspati Miśra. *Tattva-bindu*, ed. and tr. Madeleine Biardeau (*Le Tattvabindu de Vācaspatimiśra*). Pondichéry: Institut français d'indologie, 1979.

Vācaspati Miśra. *Tattva-kaumudi*, ed. and tr. Ganganatha Jha. 1896. Reprint, Dillī: Bhāratīya Buka Kāraporeśana, 2008.

Vācaspati Miśra. *Tattva-vaiśāradī (Commentary on the Yoga-sūtra)*. In *The Yoga Sūtras of Patañjali*, ed. James Haughton Woods. Mineola: Dover Publications, 2003.

Vātsyāyana. *Nyāya-sūtra-bhāṣya*. See Gautama, *Nyāya-sūtra*.

Vattanky, John. "Aspects of Early Nyāya Theism." *Journal of Indian Philosophy* 6 (1978): 393–404.

Wainwright, William. "Concepts of God." *Stanford Encyclopedia of Philosophy*, 2006. Web 2019. https://plato.stanford.edu/entries/concepts-god.

Watanabe, Toshikazu. "Dharmakīrti on False Rejoinders." *Journal of Indian and Buddhist Studies* 58, no. 3 (March 2010): 119–24.

Woods, James Haughton, ed. *The Yoga Sūtras of Patañjali*. Mineola: Dover Publications, 2003.

Index

Advaita Vedānta, x–xi, xv, 4, 6–8, 21, 25, 33, 39, 67, 69–70, 76–78
agency, x–xi, 8, 10, 21–22, 27, 43, 47, 52, 54, 56, 57, 69, 80
anirvacanīya (inexplicable nature of the world from transcendent viewpoint), 6, 64, 68–69, 76–77
argument *from delimited measurement* (for Sāṃkhya's primordial matter), 9, 13, 16
avidyā (spiritual ignorance), 7, 20–21, 34–35, 37, 64, 66–67, 69, 71, 74, 76, 78

Bādarāyaṇa, 2, 67–68, 75, 78
being a property of the inferential subject (as a basis of extrapolation), 50–51, 58
Bhagavad-gītā, ix, 1, 4, 63, 65, 73, 75
Brahman, ix n1, 1–3, 5–7, 11–12, 21, 23, 32–35, 37, 39, 63–64, 66–71, 75–76, 78, 81
Brahma-sūtra, x, xvi, 1–7, 10, 13, 39, 52n11, 63–64, 66n3, 67–68, 70–74, 78
the Buddha, 45, 66; sermons of, ix, xi

consciousness, 4, 6, 8, 10, 13, 17–21, 24, 27, 31–32, 47, 59, 65–67, 76–77
creation of world: as part of a cycle of creation and destruction, 69; different accounts of within the Upaniṣads, 7, 78n8; emerging from the union of self and primordial matter, for Sāṃkhya philosophers, 9; as overseen by God, 20, 22–23, 32, 42, 44, 56–57, 67–68, 75; as possibly unjust, 72–75 ; possible motives for, 24, 26n10, 27–28, 71; requiring conscious agency, 10; theistic arguments about challenged, 79–83

debate, xi–xii, 4–5, 12, 43, 49n9
delimited measurement. *See* argument from delimited measurement
Dharmakīrti, 45–47, 79, 82–83
Dignāga, xiv, 45

example (as part of an argument), xii–xiv, 14, 18, 19, 22–23, 47–50, 56, 81–82
everyday speech and action (*vyavahāra*), 34, 36, 71

fallacies: the contradictory, xiv, 4, 17, 32–33, 48, 80–81; the deviant, xiv, 81; false rejoinder (*jāti*), 49, 82–83; lacking the property to be proved, xiv, 47, 100; proving what is already admitted, 47, 80, 82; undercutting defeater (*upādhi*, "additional condition"), xiv, 49, 52–53, 55; the unestablished, xiv, 47, 80, 82